Following God

Life Principles from the New Testament Parables and Word Pictures

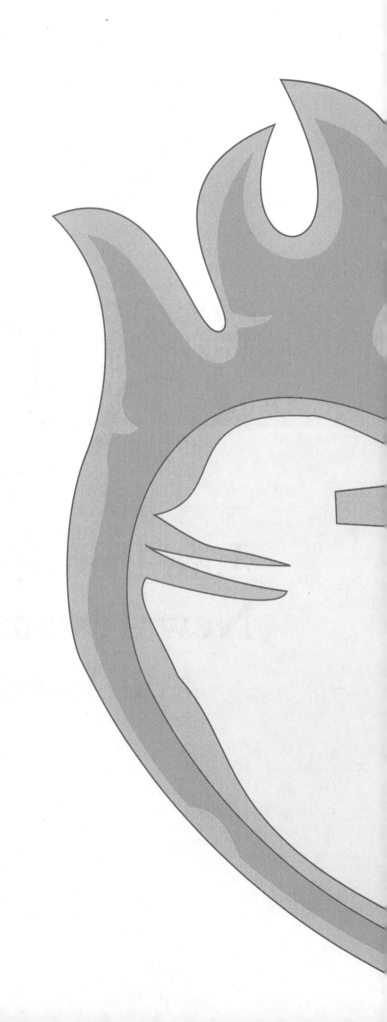

Following God

Life Principles from the New Testament Parables and Word Pictures

CHERI COWELL

Advancing the Ministries of the Gospel
AMG Publishers

God's Word to you is our highest calling.

Following God

LIFE PRINCIPLES FROM THE NEW TESTAMENT PARABLES AND WORD PICTURES

© 2012 by Cheri Cowell

Published in conjunction with the Leslie H. Stobbe Literary Agency,
300 Doubleday Road, Tryon, NC 28782

Additional resources, including small group leaders guide, available on the author's website:
www.chericowell.com

First Printing, 2012

ISBN-13: 978-089957-349-6

Editing and layout by Diane Stortz, Rick Steele, and Jennifer Ross
Cover design by Michael Largent at InView Graphics Corp., Chattanooga, Tennessee

Printed in the United States of America
17 16 15 14 13 12 –W– 6 5 4 3 2 1

Acknowledgments

I am indebted to several people who made this study possible, who sowed into my life, and who modeled parable-shaped lives before me.

First, my family—my mother, Donna, and her husband, David; my sister, Wanda; and my wonderful husband, Randy—who walked this journey with me and who believed in me long before I did.

Second, my writing friends—my awesome critique group, Word Weavers Orlando; my reader-editors Taryn Souders and Deb Haggerty; my agent, Les Stobbe; and my editor at AMG, Rick Steele—for standing with me.

Third, my mentors and professors from Asbury Theological Seminary in Orlando—Brian Russell and Steve Harper—whose willingess to pour into my life their knowledge and love of the Scriptures has inspired me.

Finally, I'd like to acknowledge the great cloud of witnesses who have gone before me—including my grandparents, Rev. and Mrs. M. E. Myer and Rev. and Mrs. J. M. Ivey, who were beautiful, living parables long before I understood what that meant. For your witness I am forever blessed.

 CHERI COWELL

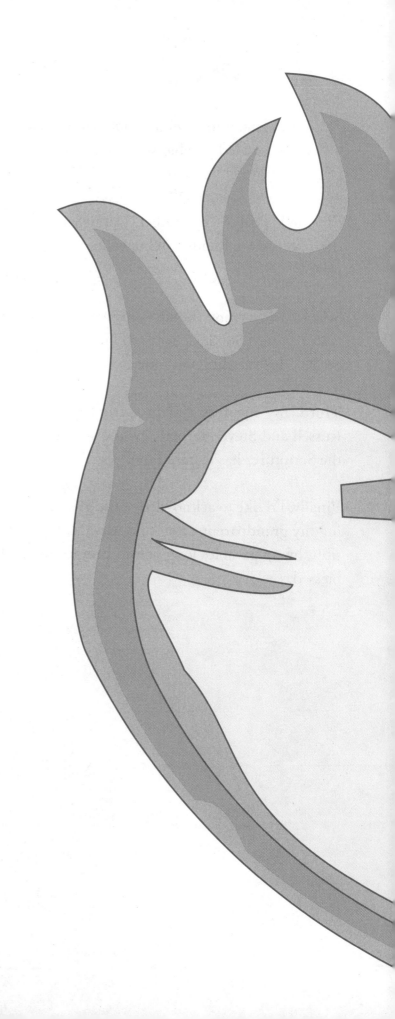

Preface

I have a little secret: I am a news fanatic. More often than not when the television is on, it is tuned to a twenty-four-hour-news channel. I love it. On the other hand, my husband can't stand the "constant warring and negativity." Randy would rather watch *The Andy Griffith Show.*

Whether you are like me and have a pulse on the economy and world politics or are like my husband and just dip your toe into world news when circumstances demand it, there is no denying our world is getting darker. A scorecard is needed to keep track of who is lobbing bombs at whom and what group is taking credit for the latest terrorist attack. The unrest is not just "out there"—it is taking hold of our own communities in the form of civil disobedience and flaring tempers. Even our churches are divided over serious issues. There seems to be no place of agreement anywhere, in any corner of the world.

In the midst of all this division and war, it seems naive to introduce a study of the kingdom of God. How can we speak of a kingdom of peace when the world is anything but peaceful? More directly, how can Jesus say that the kingdom of heaven is at hand when all around us the world is anything but heavenly?

These are the same questions the people of Jesus' day were asking. The Jews were under Roman occupation, taxes drove many into debtors' prison, and the division between the haves and have-nots was growing. The prophet Isaiah told of a day when God would *"judge between the nations, and shall arbitrate for many peoples; they shall beat their swords into plowshares, and their spears into pruning hooks; nation shall not lift up sword against nation, neither shall they learn war any more"* (Isaiah 2:4). He also prophesied, *"The wolf shall dwell with the lamb, and the leopard shall lie down with the kid, and the calf and the young lion and the fatling together, and a little child shall lead them"* (11:6). However, in light of the circumstances of Isaiah's time, those promises seemed distant.

Then came Jesus of Nazareth with the announcement that the kingdom of God was near and now. The long-awaited rule of God was at hand in the person of Jesus Christ. This wasn't ignorance of the circumstances, nor was it—as some biblical scholars have put forth—only a spiritual kingdom of which He spoke. No, this was God's direct answer to the cries of His people, His way of addressing their very real concerns.

The kingdom of God is also the answer you and I are seeking to address our present circumstances, the answer to a world gone mad. Its message is ripe for today's spiritual pilgrim, not only because of the message itself but also because of the delivery method. Jesus chose to deliver the message in parables, and as you will discover, this method resonates in today's image- and story-driven world.

Finally, just a few years ago, a campaign of "hope and change" elected the first African American president of the United States. As subjects in the kingdom of God, you and I have a "hope and change" message that is more than just a campaign slogan. It is a reality. This kingdom Jesus spoke of will be fully realized in the future, but it is also in a process of breaking in to the present. It is a promise we can hope for and a gift for the here and now. The parables tell us how.

CHERI COWELL

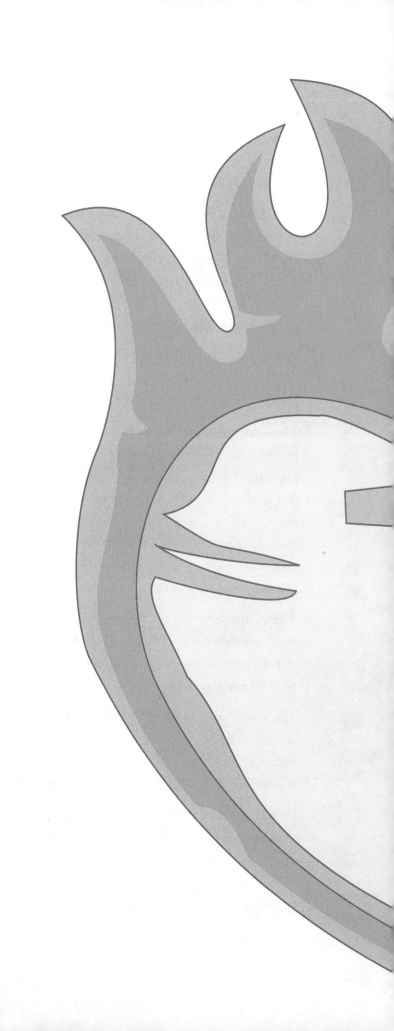

Table of Contents

Mining Parables for All They're Worth

HOW TO DEFINE AND STUDY PARABLES

PREPARE YE THE WAY

You may have heard it said that a parable is an earthly story with a heavenly meaning. This is true, but not all stories with heavenly meanings are parables. If you and I are studying parables together over the coming weeks, we need a better definition. A good place to start is with the word itself. It is derived from the Greek *parabole* that comes from two other Greek words:

1. *ballo* (verb): to throw or cast
2. *para* (preposition): alongside of

Therefore, in the broadest sense, a parable is that which is "thrown alongside of." It is a comparison.

With this working definition, we must also decide what we will include when we say *parable*. Most of us probably think of the stories Jesus told, more than forty in number. However, in addition to these important parables, there are others we might want to consider. In fact, from the outset, the Gospels begin with comparisons made by the one who *"[prepared] the way."*

📖 See for yourself in Luke 3:4–6.

📖 Now look up Isaiah 40:3–5 and record the words echoed in the Luke passage.

_____

_____

A parable is a story or illustration, whether drawn from imagination or a real event, that makes a comparison with the goal of imparting a spiritual lesson.

Luke used these words from Isaiah to help people connect the promised Messiah to the one who would make rugged roads straight. This hyperbole is a form of parable because it is comparing John preaching repentance to the man in Isaiah's prophesy who smoothes the way for salvation. If making a comparison is to be our measure of what is included in a list of parables, nearly everything in Scripture would be a parable and our study would take longer than we have time. So what other measurement can we use for determining what is a parable and what is not?

Vine's Expository Dictionary of New Testament Words defines a parable as "a comparison or analogy drawn from nature or human circumstances *with the goal of imparting a spiritual lesson*." For our purposes, let's combine the definition derived from the Greek word study with Vine's definition: a parable is a story or illustration, whether drawn from imagination or a real event, that makes a comparison with the goal of imparting a spiritual lesson. To further narrow our focus, we will examine only those parables included in the New Testament.

With our definition in mind, look at these comparisons from the first "parabler" of the Gospels, John the Baptist. Write down what is being compared.

📖 Matthew 3:10

Ax to _____
Trees to _____

📖 John 1:29–36

The Lamb of God (Jesus) to _____

📖 John 3:29–30

Bridegroom to _____
Friend of bridegroom to _____

In making these analogies, the Gospel writers use a teaching tool common in their day. Although not as common today, this form of teaching has much to offer the Bible student of the twenty-first century. It provides our image-driven minds with word pictures for key lessons in our spiritual formation. It makes the way smooth for the Holy Spirit to engage us deep in our souls. In the words of Bible paraphraser Eugene Peterson, the parables also invite us to participate in *this* God-made world where things are not always as they seem—where up is down and right is wrong and to get ahead is to end up last. Parables invite us to see ourselves in this world.

I was blessed to grow up in a Christian home and at an early age was given a picture Bible. I still cherish that childhood gem with its black and white artist's renderings of most of the Bible's stories. I was a child with an active mind, and those images provided backdrops for the stories as I imagined myself in the midst of the action. Some of the parables we will examine fall more into this category. They are what I call word pictures. They aren't wrapped in a memorable story or parable, but the images provide us a way to get inside the mind of God and perhaps see the world in a new way—a God way.

Today when I hear a parable read in church or I read a Bible story in my own quiet time, the images from my old picture Bible are the first to come to mind. Even though my present Bible isn't filled with pictures, the parables still paint pictures in my imagination. These mind pictures invite me to see myself there in the action. They also invite you.

In spite of these benefits, one major obstacle might prevent us from appropriating all the insights parables have to offer today's spiritual pilgrims. Parables use objects and situations common to the audience for whom the parable is given. But when these scenarios are no longer common, we must do a little digging to fully understand what Jesus was saying then and now. Certainly this can be said of the main theme we will be studying in these parables—the kingdom of God. Even the words *kingdom* and *of God* sound strange and perhaps come with some baggage. Some of that baggage may be our own, and some might be the baggage of biblical times. Yes, they came with baggage in Jesus' day too.

For instance, when you and I think of the word *kingdom*, we might think of dictators or people who set up little fiefdoms for their own benefit. When we add *of God* to that piece of luggage, we have God as a tyrant who rules over His subjects with an iron fist for His own benefit. In Jesus' day, however, the kingdom of God was understood as a time when Israel would finally be vindicated and God would set up His rule and no one would ever oppress His people again. The Jews Jesus spoke to understood the kingdom of God to be a time when God's enemies, and by extension the enemies of Israel, would be annihilated. So you can see that the words *kingdom of God* would have carried much weight in Jesus' day. We need a basic understanding of the people of ancient Israel in order to to fully apprehend what the parables communicated to them and what the parables communicate to us today.

Doing a Little Digging

Some of what is not readily apparent to us in our world would have been commonplace to those first hearing these parables. For instance, hearing the Parable of the Winnowing Fork, John's audience would have known a winnowing fork was a pitchfork-like instrument used to toss grain from the threshing floor into the air, where the wind further separated out the lighter, inedible chaff.

📖 Read Matthew 3:12. What is John saying about …

who holds the winnowing fork? _____

who is the implied wind? _____

what will the winnower and wind do? _____

who is the wheat? _____

what happens to the chaff? _____

With this background about the processing of wheat, what spiritual truth is

John conveying?

_____

_____

_____

📖 Let's look at another one. In Matthew 3:7 we encounter a derogatory slight by John toward the Pharisees and Sadducees. What do you think this slur means?

_____

_____

_____

What makes this name-calling all the more pointed is that in Mediterranean folklore, Arabian vipers were said to have eaten their way out of the womb, thereby killing their mothers. It was believed this was an act of vengeance for the death of their fathers who were slain by their mothers in procreation. Calling the Pharisees and Sadducees a brood, or offspring, of vipers was a way of (by comparison) accusing them of the utmost in moral depravity.[1]

📖 Jesus goes on to warn the Pharisees and Sadducees in verses 8–10. What will happen to *"every tree . . .that does not bear good fruit"*?

_____

_____

_____

What might be *"fruit worthy of repentance"*?

_____

_____

Repentance is not simply an intellectual act; it has lifestyle implications. Jesus was saying it wasn't enough to say the words or take a dip in the Jordan. The word *repent* actually means "turn around" and implies turning from sinful ways.

📖 Before leaving John the Baptist, let's look at how Jesus turned this parabolic form of speech that John used into a form of flattery. Read Matthew 11:7–9. What is the comparison Jesus is making and what is the implied spiritual message?

_____

_____

_____

As we've already read in John's own words, he expects Jesus to put an ax to the tree and set the chaff ablaze, but instead this Jesus sets spirits free and hearts ablaze. John is in prison at this point and wants to know if he'd gotten the message right.

Repentance is not simply an intellectual act; it has lifestyle implications.

📖 Read the passage Jesus quotes in Isaiah 35:5–6.

After quoting this Isaiah passage, Jesus turns His attention to the real questions John and the crowds now gathered around Him are asking. He begins by pointing to the reeds growing on the banks of the very Jordan where John preached. Reeds or rushes grew about twenty feet tall; their thin, weak blades were easily swayed and broken by winds sweeping across the desert. [To see a picture of the reeds along the Jordan, taken while on a journalist's tour of Israel in 2009, visit the gallery on the author's website, www.CheriCowell.com. Jesus knows the people are wondering if John's once-strong faith is blowing in the wind. Jesus affirms He knows *that John knows* the truth—John is not a weak reed. But neither is he a man dressed in fine clothes seeking to gain the praise of men. With satire Jesus makes the point that those who cozy up to power for personal gain are in the palace, not the prison.

I must admit that I too am impressed with outward appearances. I assume status and power equate to authority and rightness. But Jesus is saying these things can be deceiving. In the kingdom of God, those in prison often carry the message of freedom. Those who've truly been set free are often the biggest promoters of freedom. Jesus wants us to know that we aren't to judge people by their place in society or even the clothes they wear but by the message they bring.

How do you judge people? Mark one:
Are you a cover reader _____ or do you judge by the content of the book_____?

Next Jesus answers the spiritual question that John and the crowds asked and even we still ask today. Did John get it right? Is Jesus the one? Can I really put my faith in Him?

📖 How did Jesus answer these questions? Read Matthew 11:11–15.

_____

_____

_____

📖 Read the prophecy in Malachi 4:5 to which Jesus was referring.

Furthermore, in Luke 1:13–17, the angel Gabriel proclaimed that John was the expected forerunner of the Messiah who would come *"with the spirit and power of Elijah."* In declaring John a prophet of the highest order, the Elijah to come, Jesus answers the question of whether John got it right with a "Yes!" John prepared the way well.

GOD'S WAY, NOT OUR WAYS

Another way the parables speak to our needs is that they sneak up on us. Like the ticking of a clock hidden in our pillows they lull us into a place all too comfortable, the same place the Pharisees and Scribes held public sway—a place of pride. And just like the Pharisees, when we are ready to pronounce judgment against "them," we suddenly realize *we* are *them*.

Through parables He tells His unsuspecting listeners that although following the rules was not a bad thing to do, they were missing the point— the ways of the coming kingdom of God are not our ways.

The religious leaders of the day were not bad people as we often paint them but as keepers of the law they had a tough job. To aid people in knowing when they were breaking one of God's laws, the Pharisees fashioned another group of laws, or rules. The problem came, as we will see in the following parables, when instead of the rules working as a guide, keeping the Pharisaic laws became a rod for measuring who was acceptable and who was not. To these keepers of the law and to us, Jesus offers a stern message. Through parables He tells His unsuspecting listeners that although following the rules was not a bad thing to do, they were missing the point—the ways of the coming kingdom of God are not our ways.

In Matthew 9 we are introduced to Pharisees at work enforcing one of their laws—that of fasting. According to their laws, God fearers not only were to avoid eating with sinners but they were not even to trade with them, thus fully separating themselves from the impure.

📖 Read verses 10–13 and explain why you think this behavior bothered Jesus and why He chose a more excellent way.

_____

_____

_____

_____

The law of Moses (God's laws as first given) are to help God's people understand the seriousness and invasiveness of sin. Keeping the law also was to be a physical sign of the inward cleansing taking place in a repentant heart bowed before God.

📖 Thumb through the book of Deuteronomy, noting the headings and the extent to which God's laws cover every detail of life. Then read Deuteronomy 28:9–11, which explains the outcome for God's people if they followed all of these commands. From this Scripture, what do you think is God's purpose in giving these rules?

_____

_____

_____

As explained in Deuteronomy, separating ourselves from sinners is not to be an indictment on the outsiders. Nor is it to be a way of remaining pure— that was always and still is an inside job. God's people are to witness to the world, requiring us to hang out there. We are to influence the world, not be influenced by it. By following God's laws, God's people would be blessed, and all other nations would fear (respect) them and their God. In this parable, Jesus makes it clear: God's people missed the point. To add an exclamation mark to this message, Jesus said in essence, "I haven't come for you, anyway. I came to heal the sick and show mercy, as is taught by the prophets like Hosea."

📖 Read Hosea 6:1–6, then record the quote from verse 6.

_____

_____

_____

What point does Hosea make (and Jesus reiterate)?

_____

_____

_____

The people of Israel said they loved God and made sacrifices to Him according to the laws, but their hearts and lives did not reflect the love they professed. Their sacrifices and pronouncements were like the morning dew that vanishes with the heat of the sun. Jesus is telling His Jewish audience that God is not impressed with their offerings because they missed the point of the commandments.

How do we make sacrifices and profess our love for God but demonstrate otherwise in our hearts and lives?

_____

_____

_____

_____

I am a doer. I always have a to-do list a mile long. I'm also a giver. I am happy to make sacrifices to support you, especially when you are doing something for the kingdom. However, there is a slippery slope when these two traits combine. My to-do list combined with my willingness to sacrifice can make me a martyr for God. I make sacrifices and profess my love for God while doing so with a look-at-me-and-what-I'm-doing attitude, and God is not impressed. If you struggle with martyrdom, share with God your desire to sever the ties between your to-do list and your "ta-da!" attitude.

_____

_____

_____

_____

With a touch of cynicism, Jesus concludes this parable by saying in essence, "But you knew that since you estimate yourselves to be righteous." Jesus' words must have stung—and they still sting us today.

Martyrdom in the face of intolerance is a compassionate quality but for spiritual aggrandizement it is really a form of selfish suffering.

MORE OF GOD'S WAY

A parable's setting can give us some clues for interpretation, a very important step in parable mining. Often the context or setting changes how we interpret certain aspects of a parable, and this is especially the case with the Parable of the Bridegroom. Jesus is at a huge feast thrown by Matthew, the tax collector It is a sort of good-bye feast for Matthew's family and friends, as Matthew would soon be leaving to join Jesus in His mission. However, Jesus sees things differently. In His eyes, He is at a feast celebrating Matthew's union with himself, the Christ. It was a wedding feast, if you will. When John's followers show up, they want to know why Jesus didn't follow the Pharisaic fasting laws as their leader did. Borrowing from John the Baptist's own parable of the bridegroom, Jesus makes His point.

📖 Read Matthew 9:14–17. What is Jesus' message?

_____

_____

_____

_____

Here Jesus connects all these concepts together. Matthew has unknowingly hosted Christ's wedding feast. His bride, the new *ecclesia,* or church, being formed with both saints and sinners, is present. The guests have arrived and fresh wine, a new way, is being served, requiring new clothes and not simply patches on the old.

The Pharisees are not the only ones unhappy with Jesus' choice of dinner companions. John's followers believed that it was only in following the old Pharisaic laws that they'd be properly dressed for this wedding feast, and that included whom one ate with. Because they were so focused on the laws, they were unable to drink in this new wine of celebration. Jesus' parable was an invitation to join this new way of living—a kingdom way.

I tend to be a rules follower. My husband is always saying, "Cheri, no one can live up to your expectations, not even you." This is something I constantly struggle with because, when I get caught up in the checklist, I often miss the important things. I miss people and stories, I miss hurts and needs, and most importantly, I miss God. John's followers weren't bad people. They simply missed God because they were too focused on their checklist.

Are you a checklist person? If so, the next time you pull out that list, imagine the first item like this:

☐ Enjoy the party

What does this mean to you?

_____

_____

_____

When I get caught up in the checklist, I often miss the important things. I miss people and stories, I miss hurts and needs, and most importantly, I miss God.

_____

_____

Some in the crowd began to understand, but others still sought their own ways. As we see in the next parable, recorded both in Matthew 11 and Luke 7, again the example is a wedding, but this time it is children playing street games.

📖 Read Luke 7:31–35, which follows Jesus' endorsement of John that we read yesterday. What were the children saying? How does it compare with the reaction Jesus and John received?

_____

_____

_____

_____

Jesus compares the people of this generation to two squabbling children who refuse to join in the games because the others won't play by their rules. Although I'm no longer a child, that innate sense of fairness still causes me to shout "That's not fair!" when I feel slighted or when someone gets ahead not playing by the rules.

Neither the rules-following John nor Jesus with his mercy and love fit what this generation wanted to see. They were looking for a particular kind of Messiah with a particular message, and this Jesus was not him. They were like children complaining that God's plan is not going according to their demands and expectations. They wanted to know, _How will we know which ways are God's?_

Jesus tells them, and us, that the new godly lives we adopt are like the children wisdom births, and when we see these "children" in our lives and in the lives of others, we can identify the parent as God's wisdom. These three parables drive home one simple truth: God's way is not what we think; God's way, this new kingdom way, is revealed by changed focuses and lives. In prayer, ask God's forgiveness for any stubbornness of your own heart and for demanding your own way instead of seeking His. Ask Him to show you what moves He wishes to teach you through this study. Record them here as He reveals them to you.

_____

_____

_____

_____

_____

_____

_____

_____

God's way, this new kingdom way, is revealed by changed focuses and lives.

CHANGE OF FOCUS

Often we miss the meaning of parables because we read them as isolated stories. However, just as events in our own lives would appear meaningless or unimportant outside of their context, parables are told in the context of another story being told. Where they are in relation to other stories, and also within the grand story itself, is significant to our understanding. Such is the case with the parables we will examine today.

With the multiplication of the Pharisaic laws, more and more Jews were found violating one of God's laws. This forced the Pharisees to enact more laws to combat the lawlessness. This never-ending cycle created in God's people a self-focus rather than an outward focus. It caused them to fixate on the rules, rather than on the One who rules. This was not the way it was supposed to be, so Jesus tells a series of three parables that at first glance appear unrelated. Yet, through Christ's mastery, this seemingly unrelated mix of metaphors all melds into one unified message—the futility of an earth-centered life.

📖 Read Matthew 6:19–20 and answer the following questions (be as specific as possible):

What do moths do to a garment?

_____

What does rust do to a metal object?

_____

Both moths and rust eat away from the exterior to the interior. The thieves, rather than seeking imperishable things, take perishable treasures. Jesus is making it clear that we are to fix our hearts on the things that matter to God. These treasures may not make us wealthy according to the world's standards, but they will be safe from decay and loss. How will we know when we're focused on the things that matter to God?

📖 Read Matthew 6:22–24.

Jesus says the eye is the lamp, not the light, of the body. Think about this analogy. How might the eye function as a lamp for the body?

_____

_____

_____

The light is not in the eye, but the eye uses the light to interpret the world. Building on the popular assumption of the day that the eye was a window to one's heart, where it was believed the soul resided, Jesus creates a double contrast. First, a healthy eye, which is a sign of one who is generous, is contrasted with the unhealthy eye, symbolic of one who is possessive or stingy. The implication is that the one with a healthy eye properly refracts light and therefore properly interprets the world, thereby causing him to place his

> **Jesus is making it clear that we are to fix our hearts on the things that matter to God.**

possessions in the proper place. But the one with the clouded, unhealthy eye cannot see clearly, and therefore makes poor decisions about his earthly treasures.

Following this great illustration, Jesus adds the second comparison, that of the two masters and a divided heart. Jesus makes it clear: we cannot serve both God and money. It is true that where our heart is there also is our treasure. Likewise, how we look at the world and its treasures tells us a lot about the light, or lack of it, in our souls.

Jesus closes this triple point with a favorite among parable lovers. Perhaps it's because it touches on a subject all of us can relate to—worry. But worry is not the main point of this parable. This parable summarizes and completes the other two by planting a huge warning sign in the middle of the road. Worry is not the problem; it is a symptom of a heart bent in the wrong direction.

📖 Read Matthew 6:25–34, noting how many times the word *worry* is used.

That's a whole lot of worrying. We used to tease my mother-in-law that if she didn't have something to worry about, she'd make something up. Does this describe you? When our thoughts and energies are focused on getting things, keeping things, and having enough things, we enter into a vicious cycle. This cycle can become a way of life—a draining way of life. My mother-in-law grew up during the Depression in New York City, where she witnessed the depths of that despair. Although she had much later in life, the fear of not having enough controlled her. First Timothy 6:10 tells us that the love of money is *"a root of all kinds of evil."* When we love or have a deep affection for money, evil gets under our skin and invades our thoughts, causing us to worry and fret.

Jesus wants us to know the service of mammon always produces anxiety. Here the Greek word *merimnao,* translated "anxiety," shares the same root as the word that can also be translated "worry." *Merimnao* means "distracting care." Worry distracts us from focusing on the things that really matter, the kingdom things. If we are anxious, worrying about this situation or that possibility, our fear is evidence of an unhealthy eye, a focus on worldly treasure rather than heavenly wealth.

So how do we regain a proper focus? Jesus gives us the answer in verse 33. Write it out.

_____

_____

_____

_____

This isn't the prosperity gospel in which we take the Scripture to promise us great prosperity if we [fill in the blank]. We might glean this if we take these parables independently, however, taken together they show us clearly that Jesus is not saying "Focus on the kingdom things and you'll also get all the stuff." On the contrary, Jesus is saying we are to put our focus on what matters to God in His kingdom, and when our hearts are a mirror image of His, we will receive what our hearts desire.

Worry is not the problem; it is a symptom of a heart bent in the wrong direction.

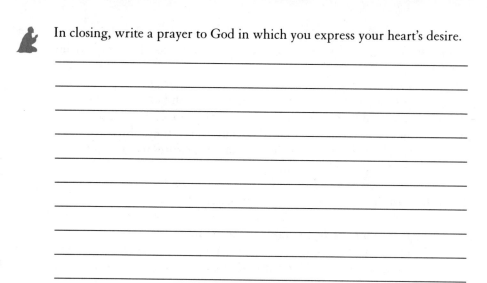 In closing, write a prayer to God in which you express your heart's desire.

_____

_____

_____

_____

_____

_____

_____

_____

_____

_____

Hidden and Yet Revealed

QUESTIONS OF HIDDENNESS AND THE MESSAGE REVEALED

Hidden and Yet
Revealed

DAY ONE

EARS TO HEAR

A key principle to parable reading is the often-misunderstood concept of hiddenness. Many have said that Jesus teaches in parables to confound the wise and keep things hidden from those who have deaf ears and blind eyes.

📖 Read Matthew 13:10–15 and explain why the people do not hear and cannot see.

_____

_____

_____

Note midway through verse 15 the word *otherwise* (NIV). This is a pivotal word similar to the *therefore*, and its presence designates a shift. Verse 13 in the New International Version begins, *"This is why I speak to them in parables,"* and then goes into detail describing those who cannot hear or see spiritual truths. Next is the big shift at the word *otherwise*. Jesus is saying that He speaks in parables to change course, to soften hardened hearts, to unclog closed ears and open closed eyes. Parables are a way to invite otherwise proud people to see themselves differently. Jesus doesn't speak in parables to keep things hidden from anyone; He speaks in parables to open hearts to the Spirit of the living God.

In this rewriting of the passage from the New International Version, insert your name or the pronouns *I*, *me*, or *my* where appropriate.

This is why [Jesus] speaks to _____ in parables:
Though seeing, _____ do not see;
though hearing, _____ do not hear or understand.
In _____ is fulfilled the prophecy of Isaiah:
" _____, (insert your name) _____ , will be ever hearing but
never understanding; _____, (insert your name) _____ ,will be
ever seeing but never perceiving. For _____ heart has become calloused;
_____ hardly hear with _____ ears, and _____ have closed _____ eyes.
Otherwise [this is why my Lord speaks in parables, so] _____, (insert your
name) _____ , might see with _____ eyes, hear with
_____ ears, understand with _____ heart and turn, and [be] healed."

📖 What does Psalm 40:6 say God has done to our ears?
_____

Once again, Eugene Peterson provides us some insight. He says that what
the translators have rendered *opened* or *pierced* literally means "ears thou
hast dug for me." Peterson compares our stonelike ears to hardened hearts
in need of a holy pickax so we might really hear what God is saying.
Parables are the pickax in God's hands, "digging ears in our granite block-
heads." [2]

I am the strong, bull-headed personality. I am a natural leader with an opinion on everything. When I take personality tests, I am always an off-the-
chart choleric, or a strong type A. However, my friends tell me I am the
nicest choleric type A personality they know. In fact, one of my friends says
I'm a reformed choleric. I laugh when they say these things because it has
taken years of chiseling and pickax work in God's workshop to shave off
those sharp edges. I've had to learn how my words were received by other
personalities, and how my get-it-done attitude came across as bull-in-the-
china-shop. In the meantime, I've also learned just how thickheaded all of
us with the varying personalities can be. Perhaps that is why I am thrilled
and honored to be writing this study on the parables, because the parables
have a way of penetrating our thick skulls and hard hearts (even if yours is
not as thick as mine).

Unfortunately, there are some who simply cannot allow themselves to
receive. The Pharisees and Sadducees did not understand this Jesus and
therefore could not receive what He was giving. On more than one occasion,
they demanded proof of His identity and authority. Jesus understood they
were looking at the proof in His very presence but didn't recognize it. Just
as with His Father and the miracles He performed before the ancestors of
these men and women, some would get it and some would not. In Matthew
12:38–40 we read that even as Jesus performs one of His great miracles, the
Pharisees and Sadducees still ask for a sign. What does Jesus tell them the
sign would be?
_____
_____

Earlier in His ministry, Jesus threw the moneychangers out of the temple
and offered this parable when asked for a sign.

Jesus doesn't speak in parables to keep things hidden from anyone; He speaks in parables to open hearts to the Spirit of the living God.

📖 Read John 2:19–22. What is this parable comparing?

_____

_____

_____

Our present society is all about signs and proof. We leave little room for the mysterious and unexplained, which seem somehow less real, less authentic. But are they? Why do we need proof? Is proof really going to assure us of anything? Some today would argue there is no such thing as proof, because in the end it is all just a matter of faith. What do you say? Are you someone who needs proof, or consistently walks in faith, or are you somewhere in between?

_____

_____

_____

Jesus turns the tables on this earlier crowd needing proof when He compares the adulterous generation in Nineveh to the one standing before Him.

📖 Read Matthew 12:41–42. What is Jesus' message to these unbelievers?

_____

_____

_____

Unlike the Ninevites who were repentant when they heard Jonah's message and testimony, these religious leaders are unmoved at the signs they see in Jesus. They are not only blind, but also insulting. He then adds, "The queen of Sheba will also stand up against this generation on judgment day and condemn it, for she came from a distant land to hear the wisdom of Solomon. Now someone greater than Solomon is here—but you refuse to listen" (Matthew 12:42 NLT). Jesus stops. He does not go further. But we know _they_ didn't stop until they finally demanded His life.

Conversely, giving His life was what Jesus came to do.

📖 If you can hear, read Matthew 13:16–17 as a song of praise to Him who has dug out your ears as Eugene Peterson describes it. Invite Him to continue His excavations so you might hear all He has to tell you.

FISHING TACKLE

When a parable occurs in more than one Gospel, it is imperative that we examine the similarities and differences. One such parable event occurs within what we refer to as the calling narratives. Parable events are real events. As in the case of other parable events Jesus uses this actual event to make a parable point using a word picture. The parable event of the calling of the disciples is shared in all four Gospels.

Matthew and Mark are essentially the same, so we will compare the one in Mark 1:16–20 with the one in Luke 5:2–11.

📖 Read them and begin by filling in the first three columns in the chart below.

Parable of the Fishers of Men	Matthew 4:18–22 Mark 1:16–20	Luke 5:2–11	John 1:35–42
What is the setting?		Jesus teaches first, then calls	John's disciples spend day with Jesus
Who is called, and when?		Peter (maybe Andrew), James, John called together	
Is there a miracle?	No miracle associated with this calling		No miracle associated with this calling
The words of the call	Come, follow me. Now you will fish for people.		Come, and you will see.
What was their response?		They left nets and father to follow.	

Now compare these to the calling as recorded in John 1:35–42 and fill in the last column.

In the first two Gospels the disciples—Matthew and Mark—are called in pairs from their boats while fishing on the Sea of Galilee. There is no miracle; they are simply called to "come follow" and Jesus will make them fishers of men. In response, they drop everything and follow. In Luke's version, Jesus is first teaching from a boat and the fishermen are cleaning their nets. He then performs the miracle with Peter and the fish. Because of the miracle, Peter, James, and John follow Jesus and become fishers of men. However, in the last Gospel, that of John, the story is very different. Andrew and another unnamed follower of John the Baptist spend the day with Jesus after He invites them to "come and see" where He is staying. Andrew then tells his brother Simon that they found the Messiah. When Simon comes (and, we assume, agrees to follow), Jesus changes his name to Peter.

What happens with most Bible students is we get bogged down in the differences. We want to know which one is the real one. Yet as good Bible students, we must remember that the point of a parable is not to impart historical fact. By example, some of us know the day and time when Jesus called us. We know where we were, what happened before and after, and how we responded. On the other hand, some of us find those details to be a little fuzzy. All we know is that we were called and now we belong to Jesus.

"'Come, follow me,' Jesus said, 'and I will send you out to fish for people.' At once they left their nets and followed him."

Mark 1:17–18 (NIV)

The point of these four parables is that the disciples were called right where they were, in the midst of everyday life. The point is, these men were ready and when they were called, they came. The point is, they left everything and followed Jesus.

These were simple fishermen with spiritual lures. They had their spiritual hooks in the water, trolling the spiritual seas. They were spiritually hungry and were looking for the big catch—the Messiah. Because they had their eyes and hearts open, when Jesus called they were ready. In turn, Jesus sends you and me out to fish for men and women with spiritual lures. Like Jesus did when He caught Peter, Andrew, James, and John, we are looking for the fish that are biting, the ones who are hungry. In this particular catch, Jesus wasn't looking for *all* fish. When He caught these four, it is safe to assume these were the four who He intended to catch at that time. What does this tell you about how you and I ought to fish?

_____

_____

_____

_____

It is easy to look at a world full of fish and feel overwhelmed with the task of reaching all of them. However, Jesus' example shows us that if we reel in those who are most hungry, the fish who are biting, we have done our job.

What are the spiritual lures Jesus used, and what might those lures be for us today?

_____

_____

_____

Jesus invited people to join Him in His mission. He said, "Come, follow me" and do what I'm doing. Sometimes I think we make this too difficult. We think we have to deliver the whole meal, from appetizer to dessert, all at once. But Jesus used a tiny hook and a worm. It took three more years to deliver the rest of the meal. Are you trying to deliver the whole meal to those you are witnessing to, or just a taste to entice? How does today's look at the calling parables change the way you will lure others to Christ?

_____

_____

_____

NARROW AND HIDDEN

You may wonder how anyone ever finds and enters the kingdom gates if the lure is small and not everyone is hungry. I've often wondered that. The task for us as God's fishermen seems too big, and if

It is easy to look at a world full of fish and feel over-whelmed with the task of reaching all of them. However, Jesus' example shows us that if we reel in those who are most hungry, the fish who are bit-ing, we have done our job.

Hidden and Yet Revealed

DAY THREE

we can't use trolling nets to scoop up as many people as we can at one time, how will we ever reach all the people in this world? The situation becomes even more dire when we read this next parable.

📖 Read the Parable of the Narrow Way in Matthew 7:13–14 in the New International Version. Fill in the blanks.

Wide is the _____ and _____ is the road that leads to _____, . . . but _____ is the gate and _____ is the way that leads to _____.

How many people find the narrow way? _____

Although we may want to save the whole world, the reality is that few will choose this path. The sad truth is, we aren't looking for every fish in the sea, just those who are hungry. The wide gate and broad road are crowded with people. It is where the action is, and its temptations are great. But that pathway is meaningless and empty and eventually leads to destruction. You and I are called to wander down this path seeking those who are looking for another way. This parable reminds us that there won't be many, but to those who are actively looking, we can show the narrow way that leads to life.
In the last of His public addresses, Jesus is speaking to a few Greeks who had converted to Judaism. While in Jerusalem to celebrate the Passover, they requested to meet with Jesus. Possibly seeing these men as firstfruits of the new kingdom to come, Jesus makes His mission clear by creating another metaphor from a common grain of wheat.

📖 Read John 12:20–24 . How does Jesus' use of this metaphor make His point? In what ways does the single grain (*seed* in the NIV) represent what is to occur in the coming days?

_____

_____

_____

_____

First the seed had to be hidden in the ground, to die before bursting through the earth's crust and forever releasing life-giving power for the crops to come.

The term *seed* was pregnant with meaning for the nation of Israel. To the great patriarch, Abraham, God made the promise that through Isaac, Abraham's seed, God will give the promised land (Genesis 12:7). That seed grew into a nation, and now in their midst lived the fulfillment of that covenant promise, the seed of promise, Jesus. Through this seed the nation of Israel would finally become the blessing they were intended to be to all people. But first the seed had to be hidden in the ground, to die before bursting through the earth's crust and forever releasing life-giving power for the crops to come. The point is clear: one seed can yield a harvest, but only if it dies.

📖 Look up the following passages and answer the questions:

Revelation 5:9-10. When is the kingdom of heaven established?

_____

_____

Luke 17:20–21. Where is this kingdom?

_____

_____

Keeping in mind the parable word picture of the hidden seed from John 12:24, answer this question: If the kingdom of heaven is given life by the shedding of blood at Christ's death (the answer from Revelation 5:9-10), and if the kingdom of heaven is within men and women of faith (the answer from Luke 17:20-21), what must we do to bring the kingdom of heaven out from within our hearts and into the world?

_____

_____

_____

Following this parable word picture Jesus answers this question.

📖 Read John 12:25-33 where He foretells of his death, burial, and His "lifting up" when once and for all He will draw all people to himself. Next, read the response Jesus received in John 12:34. Summarize that response.

_____

_____

_____

Unless the kernel (Jesus) falls to the ground and dies, unless He dies and is buried as a seed hidden in the ground, that single seed cannot become many seeds (the kingdom of heaven hidden in you and in me). And just as Jesus had to die, we too must die. We must die to our selves, our own ways, and our selfish pride so that the seed of kingdom of heaven hidden in our hearts might burst forth into full bloom and cover the earth. Few will choose this narrow way, but for those who do, Jesus offers a promise.

📖 Read John 12:35-36 and record the promise.

_____

_____

_____

After making the promise, the scripture tells us Jesus left and hid. Within these few words lie two truths about the narrow and hidden way. First, the way is narrow and often lonely. At times we will be asked to go where no one else is going, to walk upstream, to fish in the lake where no one else is fishing. The path Jesus walked was a difficult narrow road, and our path may also be difficult and narrow. Second, even when we shout to the highest the Good News of the Gospel, for many that message will remain hidden. It is not their time. In hindsight, we can see why Jesus did not simply reveal himself to everyone right then and there. But the disciples must have wondered why Jesus wasn't revealing himself to these people like He had to them. You and I may wonder the same thing. But we have something the disciples did not have. We know from the rest of the story that 'hidden now' doesn't mean 'hidden forever.' That is a promise we can hide deep within our hearts.

We must die to our selves, our own ways, and our selfish pride so that the seed of kingdom of heaven hidden in our hearts might burst forth into full bloom and cover the earth.

THE WEAPON OF TRUTH

The scribes and Pharisees tried to trick Jesus on several occasions, and each time they'd been outwitted by Him. Jesus pours salt into those wounds with this parable that summarizes His whole ministry and at the same time points a finger directly at them. As you read Matthew 21:33–46, fill in the chart below with the words listed.

- Israel, the landowner (householder)
- There will be an end to His forbearance
- Religious leaders
- Sent by God
- The Son
- Becomes a stumbling block for many

Metaphor	Does what?	Represents	Tells us what?
The vineyard	Unprepared		We will either be prepared and reap a harvest or unprepared
	Patient but just	God	
The tenant farmers (husbandmen)	Failed in their stewardship of the vineyard		Will be judged in how we lead and removed if we prove unfaithful
The servants (slaves)		Prophets	We may be treated poorly
	Is killed	Jesus	

Once again, Jesus uses the familiar language of the vineyard to make His point. For us to fully apprehend this parable, we must become more familiar with this way of living and also with Israel's history. First of all, Israel was indeed privileged by God, who is depicted in the parable as the owner of the vineyard. The people of Israel were God's chosen people. It was also well known that when a vine was given the utmost of care, it repaid the vinedresser with a grand harvest. God, as the divine landowner, took the pruning shears of discipline found in the law to His vine, Israel, for she was His prized specimen. From His watchtower, God stood guard over His vineyard, all the while building the press from which He'd collect the juice of perfection—holy lives wrung pure through the application of the law.

But it was not to be.

The landowner went into a faraway country and rented out His vineyard to tenants, the leaders of Israel. These tenant farmers were given a rich and fertile land, a vineyard ripe with promise. Before harvesttime, the owner sent His servants or slaves, who we understand to be the prophets, to ready the vineyard for the landowner's return. A little later, Jesus expounds upon the dreadful treatment the slaves received.

📖 In Matthew 21:34, who did Jesus say had sent the servants or slaves?

_____

As if that wasn't enough to make the Jewish rulers hearing this parable burn with anger, Jesus pours more fuel on that fire. He goes on to describe the tenants' abuse of their power and privilege. There was no getting around the facts: Isaiah had been beaten to death, Jeremiah was stoned, and Amos was murdered. Yet the owner was gracious and decided to send his own son, his heir. Surely the tenants would respect his son. But as Jesus predicts in this parable, that is not to be.

Just as this Parable of the Vineyard foretells, Jesus, the heir, would be slain for His inheritance at the hands of the scribes, Pharisees, and the crowds of turncoat followers—they (like us) wanted to be lord over our own lives. In a bit of verbal swordsmanship, Jesus invites the Pharisees to pass judgment on themselves: *"When the owner of the vineyard comes, what will he do to those tenants?"* They replied that he would destroy them. And so it was in AD 70 when the temple fell—the temple system and the Levitical priesthood ceased to exist. The tenants were destroyed.

What about this parable disturbs or convicts you?

_____

_____

_____

What encourages you?

_____

_____

_____

Did You Know?

EYEWITNESS ACCOUNT

"The rebels shortly after attacked the Romans again, and a clash followed between the guards of the sanctuary and the troops who were putting out the fire inside the inner court; the latter routed the Jews and followed in hot pursuit right up to the Temple itself. Then one of the soldiers, without awaiting any orders and with no dread of so momentous a deed, but urged on by some supernatural force, snatched a blazing piece of wood and, climbing on another soldier's back, hurled the flaming brand through a low golden window that gave access, on the north side, to the rooms that surrounded the sanctuary. As the flames shot up, the Jews let out a shout of dismay that matched the tragedy; they flocked to the rescue, with no thought of sparing their lives or husbanding their strength; for the sacred structure that they had constantly guarded with such devotion was vanishing before their very eyes." (Josephus, *The Jewish War, History of Rome* vol. V [1883])

CRUSHED FOR HIS NAME'S SAKE

Hidden and Yet Revealed

DAY FIVE

Today we will continue our look at the Parable of the Vineyard, this time looking at other biblical references that shed light on its meaning.

📖 Answer the following questions after reading these Scriptures, and make the connections to the verses in our parable from Matthew 21:

Acts 2:23. Who is Peter addressing in this speech?

_____

How is this connected to Matthew 21:38–39?

_____

1 Peter 2:9. Of whom is Peter speaking?

_____

How is this connected to Matthew 21:43?

_____

Romans 11:15–23. Who are the cut off and who are the grafted in?

_____

How does this connect to Matthew 21:41?

_____

Isaiah 8:14–15. Who does Isaiah say will be the stumbling block?

_____

Ephesians 2:20. From this verse, who do we know to be the cornerstone?

_____

How do these verses connect to Matthew 21:42–44?

_____

Jesus foretells what Peter confirms in his indictment of the Jewish leaders for Jesus' death. As this parable foreshadows, Israel rejects her Owner and His Son, and so the Owner turns the vineyard, or kingdom, over to new tenants, the new heirs to the kingdom—the church. This newly grafted vine will finally produce the prized juice the owner sought all along. But how will this be any different than when the vineyard was guarded by the husbandmen? The secret is found in the book of Daniel, which the hearers of this parable would have known by heart.

📖 Read Daniel 2:34–35 and record your insights.

_____

_____

_____

Immediately in hearing Jesus speak of the stone, the scribes and Pharisees would have tied the prophesy in Isaiah to this reference in the book of Daniel. What Jesus was doing in making this connection between Daniel's rock and Isaiah's stone, they had never heard before. And then to connect these references to the concept of the winepress crushing the firstfruits so as to produce that perfect juice at the hands of the new caretakers was sim-

To connect the references that begin this page to the concept of the winepress crushing the firstfruits so as to produce that perfect juice at the hands of the new caretakers was simply more than the scribes and Pharisees could bear.

ply more than the scribes and Pharisees could bear. Jesus was saying not only that they were bad managers of God's vineyard but that because of their corruption God would allow someone else to bring forth the crop from God's land. If it had not been for the crowds of pilgrims surrounding Jesus, they would have stoned Him right there.

In the Holy Land there is a wonderful place called Nazareth Village, a re-creation of a first-century village based on solid biblical, historical, and archeological research. While there on a press tour in 2009, I watched as a group of Arab schoolchildren excitedly picked olives and crushed them in the press. The costumed guides explained the process, bringing to life this parable and many others.

A question came to my mind as I watched the juice trickle from that olive press. It is a question posed to those to whom the vineyard is now rented—us. Are we willing to fall on this stone? To be broken and crushed for His name's sake? Only when the true vine was crushed for our iniquities and poured out for me and for you did the owner receive the perfect juice He longed to have from us.

In prayer, thank Jesus for being willing to become what we could not be, the broken and crushed firstfruit of the new covenant, poured out as the perfect offering for the Father.

 To help in visualizing the implications of this parable, take a walk in nearby woods and pick up a rock to represent the rock of ages. Hold this rock in your hands as you allow the gravity of the selfless sacrifice Christ gave to weigh upon your heart. Finally, invite the Rock, Jesus Christ, to be not only your life's cornerstone but also the instrument of producing in you the sweet juice of righteousness, the lifeblood of His kingdom. Allow yourself to be broken before Him, making notes here of what God says to you about what being crushed for Him might mean in your life.

_____

_____

_____

_____

_____

_____

_____

_____

_____

_____

_____

Are we willing to fall on this stone? To be broken and crushed for His name's sake?

Notes

Thy Kingdom Come

PARABLES OF JESUS

ONE DAY

Just as a story or incident in our own lives does not occur in a vacuum but rather is illuminated by the events and circumstances surrounding it, parables also are part of a larger context. Where the parable occurs in the larger story, what is said before and after, and how the writer puts parables together all add meaning to our interpretation. The Kingdom of God parables, as they are called, from Matthew 13 are a perfect example.

Many of these parables are also found in the other Gospels. Matthew includes eight parables, including a summary parable, in his long narrative. Mark includes four of the same parables scattered throughout his Gospel, and he also adds a fifth not included in Matthew. On the other hand, Luke repeats three of the same parables listed in both Matthew and in Mark but omits the others. Because Matthew's is the most complete list, we will look more closely at how and possibly why Matthew organized his record the way he did.

Matthew 13 marks a break in Jesus' ministry. Even as the crowds grow larger, resistance to His message hardens, and Jesus begins to teach in parables.

📖 Look up and record what has just happened in Matthew 12:46–50.

_____

_____

_____

_____

This was not a slight to His mother and brother but rather Jesus was seeking to explain why some would receive His message of the coming kingdom and some would reject it. All who receive His message are closer than blood relatives, Jesus tells the crowd. Matthew 13:1 records the next series of parables as occurring when? _____

Matthew wants his readers to know that this is all part of the same message from Jesus, as it occurs later the same day, outside the same house. We can almost see Jesus as He looks out upon the crowds, thinking, *How can I explain this?* Matthew describes the scene as Jesus gets into a boat and the crowd of eager listeners gathers on the beach.

📖 Let us zoom out now and take a look at the overall structure of this chapter.

Verses 3–8 (you may need to look at verses 18–23 as some Bibles don't label this parable) are known as the Parable of

_____

Verse 9 is an often-repeated phase in this chapter. Record it here.

_____

As we reviewed in earlier lessons, verses 10–17 expound on the concept of hearing.

Verses 18–23 begins with a familiar word, _____ , and gives the explanation of the Parable of the Sower, which we just read.

Jesus once again turns to teach the crowd with other parables, beginning in verse 24, in verse 31, and again in 33. Look briefly at these.

📖 Read verse 34. Why did Jesus speak in parables?

_____

_____

_____

📖 Read Psalm 78:2–3. All these things (truths) Jesus told the crowds in parables because He sought to make known what had been known but had remained hidden through the ages. This truth is contained in the parables He is telling and is available to all who have ears to hear.

Our scene now shifts. What happens in Matthew 13:36?

_____

_____

_____

📖 Verses 37–43 contain the explanation of the Parable of the Weeds. Note the words used to begin the telling of the next three parables in verses 44, 45, and 47.

_____

"Jesus spoke all these things to the crowd in parables; he did not say anything to them without using a parable."

Matthew 13:34 (NIV)

At the end of the eighth parable, in verse 53, Matthew writes, *"When Jesus had finished these parables, he left that place."* With those words Matthew puts an end cap on this section. It's almost as if we have the words *Thus saith the Lord.* In them you can see the singular purpose of Jesus' day—to preach the kingdom of God for all those who would hear.

Before *your* day is over, read the first of Jesus' parables (vv. 3–8) and its explanation in verses 18–23. Imagine yourself standing on the shore, listening to these words preached from a fishing-boat pulpit. Jesus' question still remains, "Do you have ears to hear?"

THE SOWER AND THE SEED

Let us begin to dig a little deeper now. We next have four parables, with the first only appearing in Matthew and the second only in Mark. Like the Parable of the Sower, the first story deals with planting and growing, but the comparison throws a different focus.

📖 Read Matthew 13:24–30.

As Matthew tells it, Jesus is continuing his teaching from the bow of the boat. This time the kingdom of heaven is compared to what?

_____

Who came while everyone was asleep?

_____

It is significant to note that the sower of the seed is simply "someone," and it is said he sowed "good seed." When does it say the weeds or tares were sown?

_____

The weeds were sown at night while the servants slept. The enemy does his best work under the cover of darkness. In secret he sows his evil seeds. Some translations use the word tares for weeds. In Jesus' day tares were commonly known as darnel, a poisonous plant scarcely distinguishable from the wheat until the ears formed. It was also an invasive plant like kudzu, or perhaps more accurately, like mint planted in an herb garden. Satan, our enemy, sows his noxious weeds in God's field right alongside the good wheat. When the servants ask how these weeds came to be, whom does the householder say is responsible? _____

What does the householder say we are to do about this (v. 30)?

_____

_____

_____

What might this tell us about the existence of good and evil together in this world, and when does it say that is supposed to change?

_____

_____

_____

The householder owner makes clear the reapers will collect the weeds, not the sowers or the servants. We may not fully understand the reasons for evil existing in this world, but it is clear from this parable that one of the reasons God allows it is that to take it out would destroy us, His good seed. *"Let both of them grow together,"* the master tells the servants.

Mark's Gospel continues the agricultural theme with the inclusion of the Parable of the Growing Seed and before the next parable, that of the Mustard Tree.

📖 Read Mark 4:26–29.

The sower, again, is "someone," but this time it is added that he would *"sleep and rise."* These two words are the same words translated in Ephesians 5:14 as _____ and _____, describing death and resurrection. So the seed is scattered, and while it is growing, humans are dying and rising to new life. In other words, the sower went about his life, day and night, because he'd finished his work—he'd scattered the seed. However, he does not know how and when it will grow. That is not up to him; he is simply to plant and go about his life.

And while he does, the crop will grow. First the stalk, then the head, then the full grain. When it is ripe, the harvest will be gathered. If we are to take these parables as a whole string of stories our Lord told on this one day, as Matthew depicts it, who are we to believe will reap that harvest (Matthew 13:30)? _____

In this instance we are not the harvesters.

What does this tell us our primary role is in the kingdom?

_____

Just as Jesus was modeling at this very moment, we are to simply sow the good seed and then go about our kingdom lives. By preaching to an audience of both those with ears to hear and those without, Jesus was saying that even He would scatter seed where it would fall on deaf ears. Jesus knew how cunning and crafty Satan would be, planting look-alike seeds in the same fields sown by His servants. With this parable, Jesus was preparing His followers for the malicious ways of the evil one, and He was enjoining them and us to stay focused on our role of simply sowing. The rest is in God's hands.

Now return to Matthew 13:28 and take note that the servants asked the master if he wanted them to uproot the weeds. Why did he say no?

_____

_____

_____

📖 Finish reading this sobering message in Matthew 13:29–30.

OUTSIDE AND INSIDE

The two shorter parables that follow in Matthew 13:31–33 form a pair. The difference is that one of them is about a man and the other about a woman. Yet in both a small beginning leads to an abundant end.

In verse 31, the kingdom of heaven is like what? _____

In verse 33, the kingdom of heaven is like what? _____

The small mustard seed sown by a man in the first of the parable pairs is the *Khardah*, the Arabic word for mustard. It is a black grain equal to the smallest measure of weight. Botanists tell us that within a matter of months, the *Khardah* can grow into a treelike shrub twenty feet high.

This imagery comes from Daniel 4:10–12, where King Nebuchadnezzar is likened to a mighty tree where birds rest in its shade and nest in its branches. If you have time, you may want to read this second of Daniel's dreams (vv. 10–17), a dream about God's sovereignty. In Daniel's dream the tree symbolizes King Nebuchadnezzar, who would suffer a fall from grace despite being the ruler of a mighty nation providing rest and security to other nations. What does Daniel 4:23 say would happen to the tree?

_____

_____

_____

Although most often lost on those of us not steeped in the history of ancient Palestine, those who heard these parables would have known that Nebuchadnezzar's "tree" was cut down because of his pride. Unfortunately, I can identify with this form of godly discipline because pride has been and often still is a stumbling block for me. My tree has fallen, and it's fallen hard. So when Jesus uses the imagery of a mighty tree to describe a kingdom, the omission of the second part of the story—the cutting down of the tree—would have been significant. The listeners would have been waiting for the shouts of "Tim-berrrr!" But this time the tree stands.

Before Jesus closes His parable sermon from the boat, He has one more story to share with the crowd (Matthew 13:33). He recognizes that His words have been heard by some and rejected by others, and this becomes completely clear as Jesus uses a familiar symbol of corruption and contamination—leaven—to make His point.

In the ancient world a small amount of leavened, or fermented, dough was kept back from baking to ferment, or infuse, the next batch. Every good Jew knew that in preparation for Passover and the Feast of Unleavened Bread, each household was to carefully rid itself of any trace of leaven. The words

---

Did You Know?

? PARABLE OF THE MUSTARD TREE

With this parable, Jesus was preparing His followers for the malicious ways of the evil one, and He was enjoining them and us to stay focused on our role of simply sowing. *"These are the visions I saw while lying in bed: I looked, and there before me stood a tree in the middle of the land. Its height was enormous. The tree grew large and strong and its top touched the sky; it was visible to the ends of the earth. Its leaves were beautiful, its fruit abundant, and on it was food for all. Under it the wild animals found shelter, and the birds lived in its branches; from it every creature was fed"* (Daniel 4:10–12 NIV).

leaven and unleavened occur 88 times in the Bible and not once is the meaning anything but evil. Finally, if the leaven is evil, the woman in this story, in contrast to the man in the last parable, must be the enemy of Christ.

With this understanding about the woman and the warnings against the corruption of leaven, what would you say the woman is doing?

_____

_____

The combined message of all of these parables is this: we are to sow good seed and leave the results up to God. But while we do so we are also to beware the leaven mixed in with the good flour and the tares growing in our wheat, because even a little leaven can contaminate the whole batch.

As in the Parables of the Weeds, Jesus is saying, "Beware the corrupting influence of the leaven." Some have interpreted this parable to be about the Good News spreading like yeast in the making of bread. This positive spin neglects the context. First, let's look at Matthew's word choice. The woman in the parables does not receive the leaven as if it were something good. No, she took the leaven and hid it. Nowhere in Scripture is the act of sharing the Gospel described as hiding. Next, we must look at where Matthew places this parable. Remember, Jesus begins this discourse after seizing the opportunity to compare the inability to hear to those who were where? (Matthew 12:47). _____

He uses the fact that his mother and brother are on the outside of the house to illustrate that only those on the inside are really hearing the message of the kingdom. On the contrary, those on the outside, though they may hear the same words, cannot receive the message.

Matthew drives home this same outside-inside message in how he structures the sharing of these parables. Although Jesus shares the first four parables with the crowds, He only shares the explanation in verses 18–23 with the disciples.

The combined message of all of these parables is this: we are to sow good seed and leave the results up to God. But while we do so we are also to beware the leaven mixed in with the good flour and the tares growing in our wheat, because even a little leaven can contaminate the whole batch.

This parable reiterates a previous message from Matthew 10:16. Fill in the blanks.

Be wise as _____ and as innocent as _____.

Although you and I are sowing good seed to grow the kingdom and making bread to feed the needy—both very good things, we need to beware, to be wise and alert. In prayer, ask God to give you wisdom to know when the bread is contaminated and when what looks like wheat is really a weed in disguise.

Thy Kingdom Come

TREASURES OF WORTH

To this point Jesus has been preaching to the crowds from a boat. Now the scene shifts. He climbs out of the boat and enters the house where He is staying in Capernaum. He leaves the people on the shore to reveal previously hidden truths to His inner circle of friends.

📖 Read Matthew 13:36–43 and record Jesus' answers to the questions of His disciples.

Who sows the good seed? _____

What does the field represent? _____

Who are the good seed? _____

Who are the weeds? _____

Who sowed those weeds? _____

What is the harvest? _____

Who are the angels? _____

Note that the field in this story is defined as the world and not just the church. Although we can agree that there is both good and evil in the church, this parable does not address that reality. The kingdom of heaven encompasses more than just the church; God's reign includes the whole world.

When I think about God reigning over the whole world, I no longer think of the pretty pictures of the globe most of us drew when we were children. That big blue globe with little children holding hands around it has been replaced with images of starving children, famines, wars, earthquakes, and terrorist bombings. I think of a planet being poisoned and entire communities struggling to eke out a daily existence at dump sites outside large wealthy cities.

Jesus knew the real question the disciples were asking in their hearts. It is the same question we ask today when we look at a world filled with violence and wickedness. How can His kingdom be here and now when evil is still running rampant?

Jesus is saying to them and to us, "Don't get lost in the weeds," assuring us that God will judge evil and evildoers at the right time. Then He invites us to change our focus. This is not a story about the terrible end the wicked will receive. Instead, it is a parable of promise.

"Don't get lost in the weeds,"...

📖 What will happen to the righteous (v. 43)?

_____

_____

📖 Jesus is echoing the words from Daniel 12:3. Who receives this promise in Daniel?

_____

_____

As you receive this promise, record how this changes the image that comes to mind when you think of God's reign over the whole world?

_____

_____

_____

So the next time the wickedness in this world becomes overwhelming, take a cue from this parable and change your focus from the realities of evil to the promise of the harvest.

The next two parables share a similar theme—the priceless value of the kingdom. In the Jewish tradition, wisdom is often compared to precious metals and jewels. Likewise, in these two parables Jesus compares the kingdom to a treasure.

Look up the following verses and fill in the blanks:

📖 Proverbs 2:4–5. If you seek it [wisdom and understanding] like

_____ .

📖 Proverbs 3:13–15. [Wisdom and understanding's] income is better than _____ , and [its] revenue better than _____ .

	Who is the main character?	What is the main character doing when he finds the treasure?	What does he do after he finds it?
Verse 44			
Verse 45			

📖 Proverbs 8:10–11. Take my instructions instead of _____ , and knowledge rather than _____ .

📖 Read Matthew 13:44–45 and complete the table.

In the first parable the day laborer accidentally stumbles upon hidden treasure buried by someone else. In the second, a pearl merchant sets out in search of a priceless pearl, eventually finding one.

Whether the one who finds the treasure is working class or wealthy and seeking the treasure or stumbling upon it, the treasure is just as valuable. Both the day laborer and the pearl merchant recognize the value of the hidden treasure, and each sells all he has to claim it. The kingdom of God, once discovered, is a treasure worth all we have. It is worth whatever it costs. Jesus knows its value as well as what it will cost Him. Are you and I willing to pay the cost?

Check all those you are willing to surrender:
☐ Pride
☐ Relationships
☐ Freedom to do as I please
☐ Shame
☐ Forgiveness I've withheld
☐ Professional advancement
☐ Worldly pleasures
☐ Control of money
☐ Honor from others
☐ Pain and suffering

In prayer, offer those sacrifices to God as you thank Him for the priceless treasure He is in your life.

OLD AND NEW

The next parable, that of the Parable of the Net, is about fishing in the Sea of Galilee, a topic with which these men were quite familiar.

📖 Read it in Matthew 13:47–50.

The net is called a *sagene* in the Greek. It had floats at the top edge and lead weights at the bottom, allowing it to sweep the bottom of the sea and gather fish in masses. A drag or draw net gathered fish of every kind into its mesh (the Sea of Galilee contained over 120 kinds of fish). Who pulls the net ashore (v. 48)? _____

Like the story of the wheat and weeds, this story reminds us that as followers of Christ, when we cast our nets (or sow seeds), the results will be mixed. Being such a results-oriented person, I find this message challenging. But when I manage to focus on sharing Christ with all I meet and accepting that some of my efforts will return void, I'm a lot less frustrated.

We are told to put the good fish we gather into a basket. What do you think the basket might symbolize?

_____

_____

Based upon what we've learned about those who hear and those who don't, who do you think the good fish might be and who might be the bad?

_____

_____

The sorting process eliminated the inedible fish, or those unclean according to Jewish law. Many have speculated as to the identity of the good and bad fish, but once again context must be our guide. Jesus is speaking to His inner circle, the disciples, about the kingdom of God. He has driven home a message about hearing and responding, sowing and reaping, our responsibilities and God's, and seeking and finding.

With these lessons in mind, it is safe to assume the good fish are the ones who hear and respond and who produce wheat on their stalks. They are the ones who sell all they have for the great treasure they've found and who become members of the fishing crew. The bad fish are identified too by how they respond to the message of the kingdom.

It is interesting to note that while selection is required, judgment is not. The good are gathered into baskets and later used for sustenance. They become a part of the body of Christ, giving vitality and renewed life. The bad fish are not condemned but simply tossed back into the sea, presumably given a

Jesus is speaking to His inner circle, the disciples, about the kingdom of God. He has driven home a message about hearing and responding, sowing and reaping, our responsibilities and God's, and seeking and finding.

second chance at life. Who does verse 49 say will come at the end of the age to make the final judgment? Hint: It is not us. _____

The same language in the Parable of the Wheat and Weeds reminds us again that we are only responsible for separation, not judgment. Jesus knows judgment comes easily to us—I know it comes easily for me. However, when judgment creeps into my heart and mind, I need to remind myself that judgment *will* come, but not at my hand. And when it comes, judgment will be swift and final; those who remain unclean will suffer greatly.

Matthew's audience would have immediately understood the connection Jesus was making to His future act of cleansing—the shedding of His own blood on the altar of Calvary. Read Hebrews 9:14. What are we who are cleansed to do?

_____

The unclean fish, those not sprinkled by the blood of the Lamb, will be separated out at the end of the age. Those who have heard and understand have responsibilities in *this* age. This is what Jesus makes clear in His final and climactic parable.

Before He does, He asks the disciples a simple question: "Have you understood all of this?" We know from later accounts that despite their affirmative answer, they understood very little. Yet Jesus accepts this answer and continues with a significant *therefore*. Wherever Bible students see this word, it is like coming upon a big road sign.

📖 Finish reading Matthew 13:51–52.

Jesus is saying, "Because you've heard and understand, you are considered scribes or teachers of kingdom truths." In essence, we cannot teach what we do not know, and if we know, we must share.

The Greek term used for *scribe* is *gramma*, from which we get our English word *grammar*. Scribes were men of letters, teachers of the law qualified to teach the mysteries of the Torah, the first five books of the Old Testament which comprised the Jewish Holy Word. In using this term to describe His followers, Jesus was commissioning them to teach and unfold the mysteries of the kingdom.

📖 Read 1 Corinthians 4:1. What must those *"entrusted with the mysteries"* (NIV) do?

_____

But how are we to prove faithful? Jesus answers in this final comparison. The kingdom of heaven is like a master who shares from the wealth of his treasury both old and new things. Some of these teachings were like an old pair of jeans; their truths wore comfortably. Then there were new eternal truths that rang sweet and true to the ears and in the heart where treasure is stored.

📖 Read the following passages in the New International Version and fill in the blanks:

> *Some of these teachings were like an old pair of jeans; their truths wore comfortably. Then there were new eternal truths that rang sweet and true to the ears and in the heart where treasure is stored.*

Luke 6:45

For the mouth _____ what the heart _____ .

Romans 7:6

So that we serve in the _____ way of the _____, and not in the _____ way of the _____ .

📖 Matthew 13:53 wraps up Jesus' day in Capernaum and Jesus' discourse on the kingdom of God with what words?

_____

_____

🙏 After sharing the truth in these parables, Jesus left. He had nothing more to say. The only thing left for Him to do was live it out. That is precisely what He did, all the way to the cross. This is what you and I must do as well.

In your remaining time today, invite God to show you what He wants you to do with these kingdom truths. Record your thoughts about how can you live out the message these parables contain.

_____

_____

_____

_____

_____

_____

_____

_____

_____

_____

_____

Notes

I AM. You Are.

PARABLES OF JESUS

THE GOOD SHEPHERD

When asked to name a favorite parable, more often than not people put one of the "lost" trilogy parables at the top of the list. Because they are so familiar, we may need to do a little more digging to discover new truths in these old favorites.

Luke 15 is often broken into three distinct parables in preaching and teaching, however, let's read them as they were originally heard—as one parable in three parts, having no break, and each building and reflecting upon the other.

📖 Look over Luke 15 and note that verse 3 begins, *"So he told them this [single] parable."*

📖 With this in mind, read Luke 15:1–2. What are we told the tax collectors and sinners were coming near Jesus to do? _____

By contrast, what did the Pharisees and scribes do when they came near Jesus (v. 2)?

_____

_____

The tax collectors and sinners came near Jesus to listen. On the other hand, the Pharisees and scribes came grumbling and complaining. Sometimes I show up at church or Bible study with a right heart, ready to listen and learn. But other times, I must admit, I show up with a critical heart ready to grumble and complain.

The Lord's ways are not your ways, and His kingdom is based upon who He is and not what you expect.

The parable trilogy that follows addresses both sets of people and both positions of the heart. The three form a pyramid, with each side offering a different view of the same point—a message we've heard before: namely, the Lord's ways are not your ways, and His kingdom is based upon who He is and not what you expect.

📖 Read Luke 15:2 and record the Pharisees' complaint.

_____

Being seated at a particular table was one of the ways of identifying who was in and who was out. Like living in the "right neighborhood" or being someone's friend on Facebook, it gave one status. The Pharisees were complaining about who was receiving status and acceptance by being at Jesus' table. Jesus answers their self-righteous concerns by using the concept of sheep and a shepherd.

📖 Read Luke 15:4–7.

Immediately, the Pharisees and scribes would have connected this imagery to the two contrasting shepherds presented in Ezekiel 34. Quickly scan this chapter.

In Ezekiel 34:1–10 the false shepherds of Israel had not *"strengthened the weak," "healed the sick," "bound up the injured,"* or *"brought back the strayed"* (v. 4). By contrast, in verses 11–31 we read of the true shepherd, who will *"seek the lost, and . . . .bring back the strayed"* (v. 16). In addition, we read that God will judge the shepherds who failed to care for the sheep. When Jesus asks, "Which one of you, having a hundred sheep, will care as much for the lost ones?" the indictment is clear.

To those of us who feel we are safe in the fold, Ezekiel 34:20–22 offers words of caution. Summarize them here.

_____

_____

_____

When I read this, all I can say is "Lord, have mercy," for each of us at times has butted the weak with our horns. Mark all the ways you have intentionally or unintentionally not cared for the weak.
- ☐ Not always shared my blessings
- ☐ Sought my own rights at the expense of others
- ☐ Not always used my power to empower others
- ☐ Sometimes stepped on others "to climb the ladder"
- ☐ Didn't present the full truth when it would have benefited another but cost me

If Jesus had left the story there in verse 4, this would have been a depressing word. Instead this parable and the two that follow have a different focus. In fact, they are an invitation—an invitation to joy!

📖 Continue reading this parable with Luke 15:5–6. The shepherd searches until he finds the lost sheep and then he does two things. One answer is found in verse 5 and the second is in verse 6.

First, the shepherd

_____

Second, the shepherd _____

_____

The shepherd rejoices and then calls his friends to join him in the rejoicing. This is an invitation to join in the party. Jesus longed for the Pharisees and scribes to see that the True Shepherd was there in their midst. His table fellowship included the weak, the sick, the injured, and the lost, just as Ezekiel had promised. Jesus was saying, "Rejoice with me, for I have found my sheep that were lost." But rejoice they could not, for their sense of righteousness was too great.

How often does my own sense of righteousness prevent me from celebrating God's goodness to those I don't deem as deserving? Whom in your own life do you label undeserving but God may be whispering to you, "Go and find"? Record their names here and pray for their rescue.

_____

_____

_____

_____

_____

> *How often does my own sense of righteousness prevent me from celebrating God's goodness to those I don't deem as deserving?*

The parable also presents us with another question. Who sits at our tables? Do you include among your friends those who are considered by others as outside the acceptable?

📖 Read the Parable of the Lost Coin in Luke 15:8–10.

As in the previous parable, we are cautioned against seeing ourselves as the ones being sought. In these three parables, we are the seekers. Let us remember, Jesus is addressing the question of the Pharisees, "Why is He eating with sinners?" In doing so He likens them and us to a poor woman who loses one of her ten coins.

A *drachma* or coin was about the equivalent to a day's wage. Houses were small with small windows and stone floors with many crevices, and were poorly lit. Clearly the woman valued the single silver coin because she used precious oil to light the lamp and search for the coin until she found it.

When she called her friends, what did she say (v. 9)?

_____

_____

These are the same words the shepherd used. "Rejoice with me," Jesus says. Joy is to be a hallmark of the Christian's life. How often do you get together with fellow believers just to celebrate the goodness of God?

THE COMPASSIONATE FATHER AND TWO LOST SONS

Although this parable is often called the Parable of the Prodigal Son, it is interesting that Scripture does not use the term *prodigal*. Instead the title given by Luke places the focus on the "lost" son, but which one? We often focus on the younger son, lost through willful acts of dishonor and selfishness. But the older son, the one who stays by his father's side, is just as lost as his younger brother. He is lost in anger, envy, and a sense of entitlement.

Read the first part of this story in Luke 15:11–24.

Early in my career, I served several churches as director of youth ministries. There is no comparison to the joy a child can bring or the pain they can cause. It's one thing to lose a sheep from one's flock or one-tenth of one's wealth, but it's quite another to lose a child. There are not any good parents I know who, when their children make poor choices, don't long to see them return.

Some point to the fact that in the first parable the shepherd searches for his lost sheep and in the second the woman searches for the lost coin, but in this one the father is not said to be searching. But every parent reading this knows that is not the case. If searching and finding would bring back a lost child, they'd do that in a heartbeat. However, that is not how it works with wayward children. They must find their own way home—they must "come to themselves" as this parable says it. All a parent can do is pray and wait, and this is what this father is doing—praying and waiting and searching his heart.

Verse 20 tells us what about the father's waiting?

_____

_____

We don't know how long it had been since the son had left, but we know the father was expecting his son's return. While he was a long way off, the father saw him.

Sometimes those we love are a long way off even though they are close. The addicted, the depressed, and the sin-soaked may be physically with us but so far away from us and from God. We can learn from this father. He ran to his son, threw his arms around him, and the word used next is more akin to *smother*—he smothered him with kisses.

Then he wrapped him in the best robe, put the family ring on his finger, and placed sandals on his feet—all means of returning honor. His son had returned home with a contrite heart. He'd found himself and acknowledged his sins and was therefore made right with the family. This is often the hardest part of reconciliation. When a family member wreaks havoc and then comes home saying he or she is truly sorry, it is hard to let go of the pain that person caused. It is difficult to say all is well when inside, all is not well. The scars are still there.

This parable does not tell us that restoration is easy, nor does it say restoration doesn't require a lot of work, even some counseling. What it is saying is that restoration is the goal. Those who have sinned and caused great pain deserve, according to God's kingdom, an opportunity for full restoration. As you've been reading this, whom has God been lifting up in your mind? Who needs an opportunity for full restoration in your family, in your life? Write their names here. _____

Over the coming weeks and months, begin to look expectantly for their return. Also ask God to prepare you to deal with your pain and loss so you might joyfully welcome them home.

📖 Read the rest of the story in Luke 15:25–32 and answer the questions.

Where was the older brother when the party was going on?

_____

When he heard the party music, what did he do?

_____

When he learned his brother was home, what does verse 28 say he did?

_____

When his father heard his older son was outside the party, what did he do?

_____

Summarize the older son's complaint:

_____

_____

_____

The older brother had been out in the field hard at work when he came in and heard the party music. After he inquired whom the party was for, he became angry. No doubt he'd seen the pain this brother's actions had caused. He'd listened night after night as his father cried himself to sleep, and he'd also picked up the slack in the field where his brother should have been working. He'd been the good son, doing all the right things. Now the fatted calf was slaughtered and a party was going on—and for whom? Not for him.

If the scribes and Pharisees did not see themselves in this, they were simply blind. Reread the introduction to these parables in Luke 15:1–2.

Underneath the muttering and the finger pointing were the same sentiments of the older son. The question wasn't whom Jesus was welcoming at His table but why He wasn't recognizing them and the sacrifices they'd made. They were the "good sons." Isn't it true that we don't so much mind that the sinners and tax collectors are seated at the feast, but shouldn't they be at the children's table? Why should they be at the table of honor next to us?

Those who have sinned and caused great pain deserve, according to God's kingdom, an opportunity for full restoration.

Then our heavenly Father says to us (vv. 31–32), "This isn't about your honor." He says it to the scribes and Pharisees. He says it to you and to me. It's about joy! "Rejoice with me," He invites us. Join in the celebration. For when what was lost (even when you don't even see yourself as lost) is found, there will be great celebration in heaven.

End today's lesson by praying for the lost, the wandering, and the muttering. If you've seen yourself in today's parable as the younger or the older lost son, ask God's forgiveness and accept His offer of full restoration. There is a seat of honor awaiting you at His table.

I AM

Although not story parables as we've seen in the other Gospels, John's unique approach to the parable has endeared him to many students of the Bible. Who among us at Christmastime does not love the poetic depiction of the Word becoming flesh and dwelling among us? When we think of the kingdom of God and who sits on the highest throne of that kingdom, it is safe to assume at least one of the I AM statements from John will come to mind.

To set up what we will study, let us look at a pivotal scene in John 8. As in the other Gospels, here we find Jesus at odds with the religious establishment. First is the heightened scene of the woman caught in adultery. The religious leaders wanted to stone her, but instead Jesus shames them by revealing their own sinfulness. Then in verse 31, Jesus points out that those who continue to follow His word will know the truth and be His true disciples, not necessarily those who follow all the rules. The Jews, as John calls them, answer in verse 33 by claiming they do not need to be set free. Why?

_____

_____

_____

After some brilliant verbal cuff-to-cuff, Jesus gives the final answer in verse 58: *"Very truly, I tell you, before Abraham was, I am."*

📖 Look up Exodus 3:14. What is the name God gives himself?_____

Who God is would become apparent in what He would do.

Who is God? He says, "I am." How do we know that? He says, "Watch!" Who God is would become apparent in what He would do. In effect, John is saying that the same God who revealed himself to the Israelites in Exodus is the same God who is revealing himself in the person and actions of Jesus who is the Christ. No single word, symbol, or metaphor will do to describe this great God. In fact, it took four Gospel writers just to describe Jesus' life and what He did. In his book, John is seeking to do the impossible. He is striving to find the right mixture of symbol and metaphor to describe the I AM so *"all might believe through Him"* (John 1:7). So what did John divine?

📖 Look up the passages below and fill in the table.

Scripture	I AM the . . .
John 6:35	
John 8:12	
John 10:9	
John 10:11	
John 11:25	
John 14:6	
John 15:1	

Look over the list and circle the ones that speak the most to you. As we study each one in depth, feel free to return to this list and circle more as their meanings deepen.

The *"I am the gate"* reference comes after Jesus heals a blind man (John 9).

We have a familiar scene in which the Pharisees are furious at Jesus, this time for saying He came for those who could not see and so those who do see may become blind. *"Surely we are not blind, are we?"* they ask (v. 40)—a rhetorical question perhaps?

📖 Read the preamble for the gate statement in John 10:1–8.

Jesus is both the shepherd and the gate. It was a common practice of shepherds to lie across the entrance to the stone-enclosed sheepfold. Using their own bodies to protect the sheep from predators, they also functioned as a way to safe pasture for the sheep. No one comes to safe pasture except through the Shepherd, Jesus.

So how is it that the blind man received safe passage and the Pharisees were on the outside looking in? This parable tells us that the ones who should have known the Shepherd's voice did not. Conversely, the one whom many labeled as sinful because of his blindness was the very one who could hear the Shepherd's voice.

I have a friend who became blind later in life. One day I shared with her the amazing joy of seeing the Grand Canyon. After listening to me a while, she shared about her trip to "see" the Grand Canyon. A park ranger showed her a model, which she was able to see with her hands as he described the vastness of the landscape. After hearing her speak, I was convinced she'd seen more of the Grand Canyon than I had. I now believe those of us who can see are at a disadvantage. We rely upon what our eyes reveal. My friend, however, depends upon her other senses to receive insight. When it comes to spiritual things, she is more attuned to the Father's voice than I will ever be.

"God said to Moses, 'I AM WHO I AM.' This is what you are to say to the Israelites: 'I AM has sent me to you.' "
Exodus 3:14 (NIV)

There is another truth connected to the sheep and shepherd imagery. Since John's Gospel assumes the knowledge of the other Gospel writers, this truth would have echoed alongside the gate statement. It is found in Matthew 9:36–38.

📖 Read it and answer the questions.

Who are the sheep? _____

How are they described?

_____

Jesus switches the metaphor from sheep to a harvest. The harassed and helpless become a crop ready for harvesting. However, there is so much to harvest and too few willing to do the harvesting. Harvesting is hard work, and harvesting in God's kingdom means following in the footsteps of the great I AM. It means seeing with eyes of compassion and hearing the cries of the oppressed. It means following a kingdom ethic, which requires taking the last seat or just simply sitting on the floor. It means thinking less highly of one's self and more highly of the lowly.

📖 Look up John 1:29. Who does John the Baptist say Jesus is?

_____

Let's go back to the good shepherd passage. Read John 10:11 and write down what the shepherd does. _____

Harvesting in God's kingdom means being willing to lay down one's life for the sheep of the harvest. What in your life are you willing to lay down so others might find safe pasture?

I AM. You Are

I AM

It's hard to image a more normal relationship than that between Mary, Martha, Lazarus, and Jesus. This was a place where Jesus could simply relax and be himself. But all that changed when Lazarus became sick and died. This easy relationship became complicated.

📖 Let's pick up the story in John 11:21–27.

We do not know how Lazarus died, but one thing is clear. If Lazarus had not died, we would have doubted Jesus' authority over death *for us*. Oh yes, Jesus defeated death on the cross, but we could have easily said, "That was Jesus." Instead, after his friend spent four days in the tomb, Jesus miraculously restored life to a lifeless corpse. If He can do that for Lazarus, why not for you, me, and our family and friends?

There is a difference in believing in the resurrection of souls and believing in Jesus as the very vehicle for resurrection and life everlasting. This is what Jesus' words to Martha meant. *"I am the resurrection."* Because Lazarus was dead when Jesus called his name and raised him to life again, when we face death for ourselves or our loved ones, we can say with Martha, *"Yes, Lord, I believe."*

This same message is shared with Thomas. Jesus is preparing His disciples for His death and departure from this earth. In John 14, we read the comforting words often used at funerals about the heavenly mansion. However, these words of comfort only confuse the disciples, as evidenced by Thomas's question. Record his question (v. 5).

_____

Jesus doesn't simply know the way, He is the way; Jesus doesn't only know the truth, He is the truth. And as it was the case with Martha's question, Jesus doesn't only know how to sustain life, He is life itself. What do you think it means to know and live Jesus as . . .

the way _____

the truth _____

the life _____

> *Jesus doesn't simply know the way, He is the way; Jesus doesn't only know the truth, He is the truth.*

Simply put, this is kingdom living. *"For 'in Him we live and move and have our being'"* (Acts 17:28). Outside of Jesus, we can easily lose our way, become slaves to untruths, and live lives devoid of vitality and creativity. It is only "in Him," in His power, that we are walking in the way, knowing the truth, and living kingdom lives.

The observance of the Feast of Booths, or Tabernacles, was the occasion Jesus used to make the next I AM statements we will look at. This feast was a joyous celebration of God's protection of the people as they dwelt in booths during their wilderness journey. The celebration began with the popular water-drawing ceremony, where the water was ritually drawn from the pool of Siloam, a river of moving, or living, water. The priest carried the water in a golden pitcher to the temple, where it was poured over the altar. It was at the close of this ceremony that Jesus likened himself to living water. Read John 7:37–38 and also Jesus' response to the Samaritan woman in John 4:10. Both of these make reference to Jeremiah 2:13. In these words of our Lord from Jeremiah, what are the two sins God's people have committed?
1.

2.

When we fail to acknowledge God as the only source to quench our thirst and instead seek other ways, we soon discover *those* vessels don't hold water very well.

Check all the ways you seek, or have sought, to quench your thirst:
- ☐ Food
- ☐ Acceptance
- ☐ Status/promotions/advancement
- ☐ Drugs/alcohol
- ☐ Sex/pornography/beauty
- ☐ Shopping
- ☐ Limelight/attention
- ☐ Busyness
- ☐ _____

Unfortunately, I can check off several of these and add a few to the list. One of my biggest weaknesses is food. I love to eat. If I'm honest, eating is not only about the food. It's about filling a need, a yearning, an emptiness. After He fed the five thousand, how is the crowd described (Luke 9:17?.

_____

In performing this miracle, Jesus isn't saying we will never feel hunger pangs. He *is* saying we will never want for anything if we fill up on Him. If we quench our thirst and fill our emptiness with Him, we will be satisfied— we will be full. Take another look at your list above. The next time you reach for one of these empty calories, remember Jesus is the living water and the bread of life.

Another part of the festival's celebration—the nightly illumination of the temple's court of women with its huge candelabra—provided another opportunity for Jesus.

📖 Read Jesus' words in John 8:12.

Those who had ears would have heard the foreshadowing of the Messianic age. In this passage from the New International Version, circle and label references to the light and the living water:

> On that day there will be neither sunlight nor cold, frosty darkness. It will be a unique day—a day known only to the LORD—with no distinction between day and night. When evening comes, there will be light.

> On that day living water will flow out from Jerusalem, half of it east to the Dead Sea and half of it west to the Mediterranean Sea, in summer and in winter.

> The LORD will be king over the whole earth. On that day there will be one LORD, and his name the only name. (Zechariah 14:6-9)

We know that this kingdom is not fully realized. It is an already and a not-yet reality.

Jesus used the themes of the Feast of Tabernacles to reveal the nature and mission of His kingdom. This kingdom was present in the life of Christ and is carried out in the lives of those who follow in His footsteps. Yet we know that this kingdom is not fully realized. It is an already and a not-yet reality. The not-yet part will come when God will shelter the redeemed with the booth of His protective presence, like a hen with her chicks.

📖 Read Matthew 23:37–39. When will this promised age come?

_____

_____

_____

To close today's lesson, read the promise in Revelation 7:15 and praise God for His presence both today and in all of the days to come.

YOU ARE

"Is living the kingdom life supposed to be so difficult?" one lady asked after relating the story of her week. Her daughter had just been diagnosed with a life-threatening disease, her husband had been downsized from his job at age sixty-two (a job that carried the family insurance), and their car was in the shop for a repair with a price tag that had them questioning whether to repair or replace. "God just seems so distant right now," she confessed through tears.

Jesus knew the lives of the disciples were about to get really tough. Within hours He would be arrested and crucified. The time for teaching was coming to an end. Would they live the lives Jesus had called them to? Would they stand the test?

Because of the lack of introduction to the Parable of the True Vine, some commentators suggest that as Jesus passed through the vineyards of Kedron on His way to Gethsemane, these Old Testament references would have come to mind.

📖 Look these up and make notes for yourself:

Isaiah 5:1–7

_____

_____

Jeremiah 2:21

_____

_____

Psalm 80:16–18

_____

_____

📖 With these same references in your mind, read John 15:1–11 and highlight every time the words *abide* and *bear fruit* are used.

What do you think the word *abide* means?

_____

What did Jesus mean by "bear fruit"? _

_____

_____

To abide is to simply rest. Said another way, when you and I rest in the Lord, we savor the life-giving sap that nourishes our branches, and in turn we become extensions of that main stem. Apart from that stem branches cannot live, let alone bear fruit.

. . . when you and I rest in the Lord, we savor the life-giving sap that nourishes our branches, and in turn we become extensions of that main stem.

Jesus lists four requirements for bearing fruit. Look up the following verses from John 15 and record the requirements. I've given you the first one.

Verse 2. Be pruned by the vinedresser.
Verse 7. _____
Verse 10. _____
Verses 12, 16. _____

Resting in the Lord will cause His sap to pulse through our veins, sending us out into the world as fruit offerings. The love we offer will be a witness to the Word we have in our hearts, the tender care (pruning) we've received, and the rewards obedience brings. Therefore, to obey is to abide. To abide is to rest and in resting we will bear fruit (witness). Let me add one word of clarification. When we speak of resting in God, we are not using a modern-day definition of leisurely rest (this sort of rest would not have been known by Jesus' audience), but instead is a dependency or act of leaning for support, like in a headrest. Jesus is not saying we are to cease from work, for acts of love are the work we are to do as followers of Christ. Yet, even as we serve God by serving others we are to lean on God, rest in Him, because without Him even our acts of love are fruitless.

Jesus also wanted His disciples and us to know that it is often during difficult times when our witness is the strongest. When we don't feel God's presence, when He feels distant and unaware of our circumstances, this is when we need to cling to the vine. Clinging means submitting to the pruning, taking in the Word, obeying His commands, and loving as Christ loved.

Taking in the Word, or abiding in it, takes on new meaning when we understand just who that Word is. Read John 1:1–5, 14. When you and I take the Word into our being, we aren't just studying a textbook. The words we read contain the power to create the world, to raise Lazarus from the dead, and to transform our present reality into a kingdom reality. Let me be clear, I am not saying the words written on the page are magical, as if they can be used in some incantation. But taking in God's Word is taking into your being all of who God is. It is a spiritual exercise and therefore, the I AM statements of God are not just words on a page but living promises of the power we have to overcome any obstacle we encounter. Not because the words are magical, but because those words are God-breathed.

Fill in this table by rewriting the Jesus' I AM statements as your own "I am" promises. I have completed a few for you.

Jesus' I AM	My "I am"
Because Jesus is the gate . . .	I am protected inside the fold.
Because Jesus is the good shepherd . . .	
Because Jesus is the resurrection and the life . . .	

Taking in God's Word is taking into your being all of who God is. It is a spiritual exercise and therefore, the I AM statements of God are not just words on a page but living promises of the power we have to overcome any obstacle we encounter.

Because Jesus is the way, the truth, and the life . . .	I am assured of my destination, of not being misled by untruth, and of living life to the fullest.
Because Jesus is the light . . .	
Because Jesus is the bread of life . . .	
Because Jesus is the true vine . . .	I am able to cling to Him when life is good and when it is most difficult.

Praise God that because Jesus is all these things, you are filled with promise. These promises have been sealed with another parable image. This one came as an icon actually seen by human eyes.

📖 Read John's eyewitness account in John 1:32–34. What is this image?

_____

The descending dove was God's seal of approval on His Son's mission, His character, and His witness. This seal extends to the core of His being, which the I AM statements illuminate and consummate. When you and I cling to these promises and appropriate them for ourselves, we are sitting beneath the wings of the dove—God's blessing.

Over the entrance of the church where I grew up is a giant stained glass window of the descending dove. That window and the image of the dove was a great reminder to me of the continual presence of the Holy Spirit in my life as a believer. In fact, the dove is a word picture that signifies to all believers the gift of the Holy Spirit who appeared at Jesus' baptism and who enters the spirit of every called man and woman at their baptism.

📖 Read Acts 2:38-39 and imagine the dove of the Holy Spirit descending into your own heart. This is your promise. This is your seal of approval.

When you and I cling to these promises and appropriate them for ourselves, we are sitting beneath the wings of the dove—God's blessing.

Notes

Near and Now

PARABLES OF JESUS

IT'S TIME

I am a calendar person. I'm always planning. My husband, on the other hand, is a seat-of-his-pants person. He lives in the now. After a quarter century together, we've finally figured out we need each other. I need to live more in the present, and Randy needs to look a little farther down the road every so often. This is the same lesson Jesus was seeking to impart to His disciples and to us. The kingdom of God is both a present reality, to be lived here and now, and a future reality. It is near and now.

📖 Read Matthew 24:3 and record the disciple's question here.

_____

_____

I almost wish Jesus had said, "March 25, 2015," don't you? But even if Jesus knew the exact date and time, He wouldn't have given it, because that was not the point He was making. Instead, in Matthew 24–25, as well as in some of the other Gospels, Jesus offers a series of parables that challenge us to hold a balance between being prepared and living right now.

Scan Matthew 24:1–31 and note all of the apocalyptic language.

📖 Now read the Parable of the Barren Fig Tree in Matthew 24:32–35.

When will we know the kingdom is near?

_____

_____

_____

A peculiarity of the fig tree in Palestine is that its leaves and fruit usually appear at the same time in the spring, with the fruit sometimes coming first. All of the things Jesus warned of in the beginning of this chapter are like the leaves and fruit. They are signs that the heat of the summer is close at hand. Note in verse 33, Jesus uses the word *near*. My husband and I have learned that *near* can have very different definitions. My "near" is a lot closer than his "near." I've also learned that God's "near" is a lot farther away than mine. However, His "now" also has nuances, as we'll see in this next parable.

📖 Read John 16:20–22.

> ## Our "nows" are but fleeting. Yes, they are real, and the pain can feel almost overwhelming at times, but they are here today and gone tomorrow. That is, if we are on God's time.

What is "now"? _____

What will tomorrow bring? _____

Again, context helps us a lot in understanding this parable. Jesus is telling His disciples that the pangs of grief they are about to experience will be as painful and deep as the pangs of childbirth, but that quickly the throes of pain will be replaced by unspeakable joy. When that bundle of joy is placed in your arms, all the time in labor becomes a fading memory. Our "nows" are but fleeting. Yes, they are real, and the pain can feel almost overwhelming at times, but they are here today and gone tomorrow. That is, if we are on God's time.

In Matthew 24:26–28, Jesus assures us we will know when we need to know.

📖 Read this Parable of the Vultures. What do the corpse and vultures tell us about the end times?

_____

_____

_____

In the end of time, the spiritually dead and decaying will endure carcass-eating vultures circling overhead. When I picture this parable, I am haunted by images of the addicted afflicted by their drug of choice. I see images in my mind of drawn and hollow bodies. The vultures of their addiction encircle these spiritually dead and decaying souls. As more and more people seek help for addictions, you and I might begin to look to the heavens. When God's timing is perfect and lightening cracks the sky from east to west, I imagine those vultures running for the hills.

Lest we become weather forecasters, seeing meaning in every earthquake or natural disaster, Jesus offers a stern warning. Read it in Matthew 16:1–4. We return to the same question the disciples were asking, "How can we read the signs of the times?" When is this kingdom coming? For all of our great technology, we still can't predict outside of a few minutes or hours when disaster might strike. We are helpless to stop it. This is reminiscent of the words God spoke in Job 38:4–7. In essence God says to Job, "Who are you to question me?" Jesus is saying the same thing to the Pharisees, Sadducees, and to us. He is saying, "You can't even get the weather forecast right, so who do you think you are to ask for a sign?"

The only sign they needed, the only sign you and I need we are told, is the sign of Jonah. What do you think this is a reference to?

_____

_____

_____

For three days Jonah sat in the belly of a whale. For three days Jesus sat in the belly of a tomb. But within three days Jonah was spit from sure death, and within three days death could no longer hold Jesus in its grasp. The empty whale tomb and the empty rock tomb are the only miraculous signs we need that the kingdom of God is both near and now.

THE WARNING FLAGS ARE WAVING

Before jumping into today's parable, we must unpack the baggage hearers of the Parable of the Sheep and Goats would have come with. Look up these passages and answer the questions.

📖 Daniel 7:13–14. Who is the Son of Man?

_____

📖 Joel 3:2. What were the nations put on trial for?

_____

📖 Zepheniah 3:8. What will happen in these last days?

_____

_____

On judgment day the nations will be put on trial and the Son of Man will sit on the judgment seat. With this baggage tucked beneath your arm, let's begin reading this great parable in sections, beginning with Matthew 25:31–33.

Answer these questions:
Who do you think are included in *"All the nations"*?

_____

Who are the sheep?

_____

Who are the goats?

_____

There is much discussion and disagreement in scholarly circles as to the above questions. Some see "all the nations" to include Gentile nations, while others see this as referring to all believing sets of people. Some see the sheep and goats as believers and nonbelievers, while others see them both as believers but the goats without "fruit." It is safe to say that because Jesus did not make these points clear, perhaps we need to look further into the parable for what *is* made clear.

📖 Read verses 34–40. Of note is the word *"inheritance"* (NIV) or *"inherit the kingdom"* (NRSV), an echo of Joel 3:2.

The perfect kingdom where God will sit upon His throne and every knee will bow before Him will be our inheritance. This inheritance, however, has been parceled to us through our adoption in Christ. Our inheritance is to be spent wisely. How did the sheep to the right wisely spend their portion of the inheritance?

_____

_____

These sheep shared their blessings. They gave food to the hungry, water to the thirsty, shelter to the stranger, and clothes to the naked. They nursed the sick and visited those in prison. They gave out of what they'd been given.

📖 Read the final section of this parable in Matthew 25:41–46.

The frightening thing about this parable is that the goats know the king and yet suffer eternal damnation. What separates the righteous sheep from the unholy goats is not their profession of faith—it is their acts of faith. Many a scholar has tried to rework this parable, to make any connections to works-righteousness disappear. The problem is neither Jesus nor Matthew appears to have qualms about faith over against works. To do so here is to read into this parable that which is not there.

The point of this parable and the next two is that there is still time to get ready, but judgment is coming and what you do or don't do has huge implications—eternal implications. The goats in this parable saw human need but failed to recognize in whose image those in need were created. Perhaps they were like you and me and justified their inaction, saying, "Those people don't deserve or haven't earned my help." We don't know what went through the goats' minds, but it certainly wasn't "These are my brothers and sisters; in them I see the image of Christ." Is this what you and I say when we see a need?

📖 James 2:14–16 says it beautifully. Record your thoughts here.

_____

_____

_____

There is more to knowing the "when" of the coming kingdom; there is the required preparation. I am a native Floridian, so I'm quite familiar with annual hurricane preparations. Like the red flags that fly over our beaches when threatening weather forebodes, these three parables in Matthew wave a red-flag warning. Be wise! Be ready!

📖 Read the first warning parable in Matthew 25:1–14.

Bridesmaids were to accompany the bridegroom on the way to the wedding celebration, lighting the way with their lamps. In the story, the maidens fall asleep while waiting for the delayed groom, and when they awake, five realize

Like the red flags that fly over our beaches when threatening weather forebodes, these three parables in Matthew wave a red-flag warning. Be wise! Be ready!

their lamps are running low on fuel. The five foolish maidens ask if they could borrow some oil, but the wise women realize that if they share their oil, all ten will be in the dark when the groom arrives. So the foolish have to go out to find their own oil. By the time they return, the procession is over, the job they were to do is completed, and the door to the celebration is shut.

The parable ends with chilling words in verse 13. Fill in the quote: "_____, for you know neither the day nor the hour."

We often hear this next warning parable as a stewardship sermon illustration. However, this story is not about time, talent, or treasure, although it is closely related.

📖 Read this second warning parable in Matthew 25:14–30.

Before the master leaves town, he gives his servants or slaves various sums of money to manage while he is gone, "each according to his ability." The first two make wise investments and return their master's money with interest. The third is full of fear and allows that fear to guide his behavior. When the master returns, he is furious, because this wicked slave can only offer what was originally entrusted to him. The master takes the money from the third man, gives it to the first, and casts the lazy man into outer darkness, "where there is weeping and gnashing of teeth."

The time for preparation is now. Will you and I have oil in our lamps when the bridegroom arrives, or will we be running to the store and miss the party? When our master returns and we stand before Him to account for the trust invested in us, will we be able to say, "We've been preparing for your return; here is triple the return on your investment in us."

Besides participating in this Bible study, list other ways you are investing in the kingdom what God has invested in you.

_____

_____

_____

_____

At the end of the three warning parables, there appears to be a reckoning. At this point it is too late to change course, to get prepared, to have made better decisions. The red warning flags are waving. Are you heeding them?

The time for preparation is now!

BANQUET COSTS

Near and Now

Growing up in the church in the South meant one thing—dinner on the grounds. Literally, tables and chairs were dragged out onto the grounds of the church where the tables were filled with every fried, sauced, ham-hocked, cooked-all-day covered dish you could imagine. Every big occasion was marked by one of these supersized meals. We used to tease that one couldn't come into this world or exit it without a covered-dish dinner. So when the final consummation of the reign of God is described as a wedding banquet, I feel right at home.

📖 Read the prophesy in Isaiah 25:6.

Once again Jesus uses the familiar to make a point, although we may need a little background in ancient wedding customs to make this parable a fully satisfying meal.

📖 Read the first part of this great parable in Matthew 22:1–10.

Whether one sees in this parable the story of Christ and the refusal of Israel to heed the invitation He was offering, as many scholars do, or whether one simply takes the story as is without allegorizing the king as God, the son as Jesus, and the guests as Israel. The point of the parable is the same one Jesus has been making, namely that our actions have consequences.

How many invitations did the king send (vv. 3–4, 9)?

_____

What were the three different responses to the first two invitations (vv. 5–6)?

_____

_____

_____

What did the king call those who refused the first invitations (v. 8)?

_____

_____

> *The king sends many invitations, but at some point those invitations will end. There will be no more time to respond. The banquet will be ready. In the end, some will hear the words not worthy. How sad.*

The king sends many invitations, but at some point those invitations will end. There will be no more time to respond. The banquet will be ready. In the end, some will hear the words *not worthy*. How sad. To be worthy all they had to do was accept the invitation; both good and bad was invited.

📖 Read what some call part two of this parable in Matthew 22:11–14.

To fully understand this part, we need to understand a few cultural customs. First, it was customary for wedding guests to be given garments to wear. Also, suitable raiment was a requirement when coming before a king. Finally, not accepting and wearing the clothes provided would have been an insult to the host.

📖 Read Isaiah 61:10.

Thus the robe the man refused to wear represents the imputed righteousness that God, our king, graciously provides through Christ. "Imputed" is a big theological word, which simply means accredited or attributed. With this information the point becomes clear. We must first accept the invitation to join in the marriage feast, this grand feast celebrating the union of Christ and His beloved. Second, we must choose to put on the wedding clothes He provides, the robe of righteousness, paid for by the blood of Jesus, and in doing so God's righteousness is accredited to us.

📖 For encouragement, look up Revelation 19:7–9 and imagine yourself at the wedding supper of the Lamb.

It must be remembered that our invitation to that great banquet comes by way of a cross. John includes an interesting parable in his Gospel that makes this point, and it precedes one of the most beloved Scriptures in the whole Bible.

📖 Read John 3:14–17.

John 3:16, the *"God so loved the world"* passage, is often not read with the previous verse even though it is connected to it by the transition word *for*. That *for* means we must understand the parable to fully apprehend verse 16. To comprehend this parable one must remember the reason why Moses elevated a snake before the Israelites.

📖 To refresh your memory, read Numbers 21:4–9 and answer the question.

What happened to the snakebitten people who gazed on the image of the deadly snake erected on a pole?

_____

_____

John makes the comparison not to the resurrected Christ but to the crucified Christ, who was raised on a cross. Just as the Israelites looked up to the image of the very thing that caused death in order to save their lives, we must look to the cross, the very thing that represents torturous death, for everlasting life. In the words of John, *as Moses lifted up the snake, even so the Son of Man must be lifted up that whosoever believeth in Him will have everlasting life.* The banquet is bought and paid for at the cross.

Express your appreciation for the life-giving cross in a written prayer to God, who sent His only Son so you might have everlasting life.

_____

_____

_____

_____

_____

TAKE THE EASY YOKE

My mother loves this parable. One day during my early teens, my father came home with this prop, which she used many times at church as an object lesson. The wooden yoke, which he got from an old farmhouse, hung over our garage door for many years. Every time I drove into the driveway, it reminded me of the message of this wonderful parable.

📖 Read it in Matthew 11:28–30.

The yoke is a heavy wooden harness that fits over the shoulders of two farm animals such as oxen or cattle. It *yoked* the two animals together so they could share the weight of pulling the load with which they were burdened.

The yoke made it easier for both animals, but it also allowed a stronger beast to help a weaker one. Jesus knows we are the weaker one. He offers to take our yoke in exchange for His.

What did Jesus promise for those who take His yoke?

_____

_____

The promise of rest is an echo of the promise from the Lord in Jeremiah 6:16. What does this Scripture say is the way to rest?

_____

_____

Later, in Jeremiah 18:15, we learn specifically what made the nation of Israel stumble on that path. What is it? _____

With this background, let's now look at the context of this parable. What does Matthew 11:20–24 tell us Jesus has just done?

_____

_____

_____

Jesus is angry because those who were supposed to be "walking the ancient paths" were not doing so. In fact, they were so far off the path, they didn't recognize who Jesus was, even though He'd performed many miracles in their sight. In verse 25, who does Jesus say *"these things"* are hidden from?

_____

The wise were the arrogant. Assured of their own knowledge, they were not humble and teachable.

But not everyone was arrogant and on the wrong path, because in Matthew 11:25–27, Jesus turns His attention to those who were burdened. Who does Jesus call them in verse 25?

_____

God's children were having heavy burdens placed upon them. To fully understand this, we need the help of Peter. In his address to the council at Antioch, Peter makes reference to this parable.

📖 Read Acts 15:6–11. What does Peter say is the yoke that was placed on them and their fathers, or ancestors?

_____

Their interpretation of the law was the yoke that burdened the Jews through the centuries. In this speech, Peter is calling for an end to this way of seeing the law. Peter makes it clear that the ancient way is, and always has been, what (v. 11)?

_____

Thus, Jesus' yoke was what?

_____

Jesus offered grace in exchange for the burden our further interpretation of those laws placed upon God's children. The law was never meant to be a burden but instead was to point us toward God's grace, the ancient path that had always been there. The yoke of grace is easy, and the burden it offers is light.

What burdens are you carrying? What laws of God are you striving to follow and finding in that striving the weight is more than you can bear? Make a list.

_____

_____

_____

The message of this parable is grace. God wants to exchange our burdens for His grace, offered through His Son, Jesus. Whether your burdens are small, like a cross word uttered in anger, or a heavy burden like unforgiveness, God's grace is offered. So if you are burdened, try this exercise. Picture yourself with those heavy burdens yoked around your neck. Then imagine Jesus standing before you with a yoke labled *Grace*. Will you accept His grace in exchange for your heavy yoke? If you are willing, take that yoke from your list above and offer it to Jesus. Watch Him place your yoke around His own neck and the yoke of grace around your neck. Feel how different His yoke is compared to what you've been carrying. Then thank Him for His willingness to take your burdens so you might rest in His grace.

DIRTY LITTLE SECRET

As the saying goes, you know it is a recession when your neighbor is out of work, but it is a depression when you are out of work. The Parable of the Laborers in the Vineyard is one of the most difficult in all of Scripture. Perhaps it is difficult because it turns what we believe about fairness and justice on its head. On the other hand, could it be difficult because it turns a critical eye on a dirty little secret we all harbor?

Because this parable begins in Matthew 20 with the little word *for*, we need to look at what comes before. Peter has just asked the question all the disciples had on their minds but were afraid to ask.

Read Matthew 19:27 and paraphrase that question.

_____

Jesus answers by promising a hundredfold for their sacrifices and then adds, *"But many who are first will be last, and the last will be first."* He continues with this parable.

"Now then, why do you try to test God by putting on the necks of Gentiles a yoke that neither we nor our ancestors have been able to bear? No! We believe it is through the grace of our Lord Jesus that we are saved, just as they are."

Acts 15:10–11 (NIV)

Near and Now

DAY FIVE

📖 Read it in Matthew 20:1–16.

The owner of the vineyard needed more hands, so he went to the local day-laborer pool and hired workers, some early in the day and others at various intervals throughout the day. He promised each a fair day's wage. When the day ended and it was time to settle accounts, he chose to pay the men who worked the full day the same as the men who only worked an hour. Then the murmurings began.

When I hear this parable I want to picket the landowner's vineyard with signs that read "Unfair Employment Practices." Be honest—don't you want to join me? To add insult, we are asked to accept that this is right in the kingdom of heaven because the landowner gets to decide what is just. But somehow that doesn't make me feel any better. Often those who preach on this parable say we shouldn't begrudge God's generosity. I'm still not feeling better.

May I be so bold and propose that the Parable of the Vineyard is not about grace and God's generosity? If it were about generosity, why are these poor day laborers barely paid more than the minimum wage? If it were about grace, then why are the men paid a fair day's wage for the work done and not simply because they were in need? Why not simply give the men what they needed if it is about grace?

Evil eyes cannot see good. Evil often turns green with envy when the reward others receive is compared with what we have in our own hands.

Part of our problem in interpreting this parable has to do with an unfortunate translation. The clever rhyme in verse 15, "Or are you envious because I am generous?" should read, "Is your eye evil because I am good?" Evil eyes cannot see good. Evil often turns green with envy when the reward others receive is compared with what we have in our own hands. And why is that? Does a reward really become any less when compared to that of others? No. In fact, this parable is about envy.

Calculating what we have in comparison to what others have is not kingdom living. Instead, the kingdom is characterized by the character of the king, and our king is indeed generous and gracious, but this parable is not about God. It is about us and our tendency to envy what others have.

In verse 16 Jesus addresses the question Peter asked and with which we began (you paraphrased that question above). This parable is about the dirty little secret Jesus knew the disciples were harboring in their hearts—envy. Jesus wants them to know that the kingdom of God isn't about fairness or justice, as we often want to make it. At this point, the disciples didn't care about these things. Not yet. They were all about comparison and envy, just as we often are. As evidence, shortly following this parable, in verses 20–21, the mother of James and John asks—presumably at the urging of her sons—for special privileges for her two boys in the coming kingdom. They were in the comparison game.

The parable's purpose was to shine a big spotlight on their—and our—inner tint of green. Not a very God-like characteristic. As we learn from our post-biblical history, these two men indeed experienced changed hearts. John together with Peter played a prominent role in the founding of the church, and the spread of the gospel to Spain is credited to James, who was the first of the apostles martyred. No longer were these men's hearts green, but pure and white as snow. Likewise, may you and I not be green and envious but instead have hearts white as snow in the near and now.

I Have Decided

PARABLES OF JESUS

A HAUNTING CALL

There is no denying, the gap between the haves and the have-nots is growing, which makes this next parable all the more poignant. For as Christians who must live and work within the systems of society, we come to the questions posed in this parable with one foot firmly in this world and one also in another.

The Parable of the Rich Man and Lazarus is the only parable in the Bible where the characters have names. Some claim it isn't a parable because of this fact; perhaps it is a true story. By our definition, it is indeed a parable, and a haunting one at that.

One of the main characters in this drama is Lazarus, whose name means "God helps." It is a shortened form of the name Eliezer, the name of Abraham's servant in Genesis 15:2.

📖 With that in mind, read this parable in Luke 16:19–31.

It is important to know that the food that fell from the rich man's table did not fall accidentally but was pieces of bread used to wipe the hands and then thrown under the table. Lazarus was treated as a dog in this man's house, or even worse, because the dogs licked his oozing wounds, presumably from a skin disease.

When the rich man dies, he is buried, one last sign of honor and dignity. But that is where the man's good fortune ends. Lazarus, on the other hand, isn't even afforded the dignity of a burial, but after his death he is treated with dignity and honor by being seated next to the great patriarch Father Abraham.

As opposed to what some have said when using this parable to preach on the dangers of wealth, the rich man was not sent to Hades because he was rich.

Why do you think he was sent there?

_____

From his place of torment in Hades, the rich man looked up and called on Father Abraham to send whom (v. 24)? _____

He not only was a man of faith, for he recognized the great patriarch, but he recognized the beggar who suffered outside the gates to his estate. He even knew the man's name! This man's shame seems to be elevated a notch. It wasn't as if he had seen the need but chosen not to help. No, he not only chose not to help but to indulge himself even more instead.

This is the same message as in the Parable of the Sheep and Goats—neglect the poor at great risk. Wealth is not the problem, but those with wealth who do not see poverty and then act to correct exploitation and injustice are not using wealth rightly.

Another sad point to this parable is the great, impassable chasm that exists between the place of eternal torture and paradise. Once the rich man realizes there will be no crossing that gulf, he pleads with Abraham for the evangelization of his family.

How many of us have family members for whom we are praying day and night that they might be spared the fate of the rich man? We know there is no turning back once that last breath is taken, and this parable makes it clear—there is no changing places once we arrive at our eternal destination. Therefore, the rich man pleads for Lazarus to be allowed to go to his brothers. But Abraham explains what you and I know to be true. Read the final words again in verse 31.

"Even if someone rises from the dead." Jesus rose from the dead, and still some choose not to believe. To escape the fate of the rich man we are told in John 3:5–8 that we must be born of the Spirit. Read it and answer the question.

John compares the Spirit to what? _____

The wind blows but we cannot always tell where it comes from or where it is going, and neither can we tell who is saved and who is not. We do not know how the Spirit is working in someone's heart, and therefore we pray for all who have not openly confessed Jesus as Lord. For *"no one can enter the kingdom of God without being born of water and Spirit."*

Record the names of those family members you are still praying for and who have time to make their choice. Spend your remaining time today praying for these by their names, that they might heed the calling of the Holy Spirit.

_____

_____

_____

The wind blows but we cannot always tell where it comes from or where it is going, and neither can we tell who is saved and who is not.

A PARABLE FOR TODAY

Foreclosures, bankruptcies, and debt consolidation are unfortunately commonplace in today's lexicon. Our country has gone through a time of tremendous financial hardship after years of living footloose and free. Many of us have found ourselves in places where we never thought we'd be, buried under mounds of stifling debt. Our homes are underwater, and we see no way out.

The Parable of the Unforgiving Servant is a parable for our times. But before we jump into the reading of that parable, it must be set up.

📖 Read Peter's question to Jesus in Matthew 18:21–22.

📖 Jesus follows that exchange with this parable. Read Matthew 18:23–35.

In this straightforward parable the king essentially called in the note on the man's debt, which was considerable. Ten thousand talents equaled fifteen years of wages, a debt that could not be paid. There is no mention of how the man got into debt and no protests from the man that he did not owe what the king said he owed. The man was desperate, so he did the only thing a self-respecting man could do—he fell to his knees and begged. Surprisingly, the king relented and not only wiped out the man's debt but set the man and his family free. Freeing a slave was a form of debt forgiveness since one became a slave if one was unable to pay one's debts.

Forgiveness and debt were closely related kingdom principles. The Year of Jubilee was a liberation from all that enslaved.

Scan Leviticus 25:8–55 to get an understanding of the economic and social implications of this biblical concept. Pay close attention to verses 39–40.

So the king forgave the slave's debt and set him free, but when the now-freed slave came upon a fellow slave who owed him money (and owed him less than what he'd owed, I might add), he did not return the same charity. In the New International Version, note the same words used to beg for mercy in Matthew 18:26, 29. The freed slave threw his friend into debtor's prison, where he was assured never to have the chance to repay his debt and thus be set free.

Verses 34–35 should send shivers down the spine of every believer. For when we pray the Lord's Prayer, we are pledging, "Even as we forgive the debts of those who've sinned against us, Lord, we ask you to forgive us." God's kingdom on earth proclaims a new economic and social reality. That reality begins with the forgiveness of debts.

Who is God bringing to your mind as you've read about the forgiveness of debts? Who owes you a debt that can never be repaid? Record that person's name here.

_____

_____

God's kingdom on earth proclaims a new economic and social reality. That reality begins with the forgiveness of debts.

Then in prayer, ask God to help you forgive because you have been forgiven.

The fruit of repentance is the theme in this next parable. The Parable of the Unproductive Fig Tree is found in Luke 13, but as in our previous parable, we need to look at the context before diving in.

Luke 13 begins by telling of an incident that was no doubt the talk of the town. Pilate had massacred Galilean Jews at the ritual slaughtering of animals for temple sacrifice. All over town, people must have been murmuring about this horrific act. By the words of Jesus in verses 2–5, we glean that the prevailing view was that somehow they'd met this grisly end as punishment for sin. Jesus emphatically denounces this false theology and ends with a warning.

Fill in the blank: "Unless you _____, you will all _____ as they did."

📖 Read the parable that follows in Luke 13:6–9.

Just as an unproductive fig tree will eventually be cut down, so will the judgment of God come upon those who do not produce the fruit of repentance. What do you think this fruit might be?

_____

_____

_____

When we take the previous parable together with this one, one of the pieces of fruit we must possess is the extension of forgiveness to others. And like the yearlong reprieve granted the fig tree in this parable, when you and I see others suffering, we are to extend not blame but grace, another piece of fruit. Forgiveness and grace—fruit of repentance—may we all prove so fruitful.

I Have Decided

DAY THREE

DECISIONS, DECISIONS

Today's parable could have been ripped from the front pages of our newspapers. It has everything we've come to expect in stories of corporate greed, embezzlement, slimy and dishonest employees, and tax loopholes that allow the guilty to wiggle out of any responsibility. It's the kind of story that makes our blood boil.

📖 Read the Parable of the Dishonest Steward in Luke 16:1–9.

The CEO of this large corporation decided to do an audit of his books and found one of his employees was embezzling. It seems that in a very complicated scheme, this employee had been taking a kickback from each subcontractor in the form of a hidden tax. So the CEO summoned the employee and asked for an accounting. The employee broke out into a cold sweat. Then an idea came to him. He called in each subcontractor and offered to cut his bill by one-third, the exact amount of the kickback, if he'd write down that the company only owed him the cost of goods, minus the kick-back he'd been pocketing. The employee would take the hit, and his boss would be clean and clear. When the CEO learned of the employee's cunning, he hailed him as shrewd—dishonest, but shrewd.

I simply don't like this parable. It is a tough one to swallow. The hero in this story is a greedy, self-serving, dishonest employee. Yes, he figured out a way to make things right, but as my mother would say, "Two wrongs don't make a right."

But is that always true? Those who work in the corporate world may not want to admit it, but they get this parable. Corporate people, as opposed to those of us who live in little church cocoons, know things are not always black and white (my interpretation of verse 8). On the other hand, Christians in the corporate world know that because we didn't set up the system in which we must function, and because that system works off a very different set of principles than Christians do, sometimes we must choose the better of two evils. Now, I'm not saying this guy was a good guy, but the parable clearly teaches that when backed into a corner, he acted wisely, shrewdly, and within the system.

Verses 10–13 summarize this point. In light of the kingdom, we must be both wise and shrewd in the use of possessions. The final dictum, *"You cannot serve God and wealth,"* when separated from this context, is used to say we must not cling to our money. But when read in context with this parable, it says we must be willing to make tough choices when it comes to money and this world. Choose wisely and shrewdly!

After a series of recent storms, I visited family in south Florida. They took me out to the beach to see the erosion those storms had carved from the pristine sands. I was shocked. The boardwalk barely hung on, and all of the sand repiped from the bottom of the ocean just the year before, at a cost of millions, was now back at sea. Although the houses sat well back from the dunes, they were now in danger of falling into the ocean. As I stood there viewing the results of the awesome power of wind and rain, this next parable came to my mind.

📖 Read the Parable of the Two Builders in Matthew 7:24–27.

Those who hear and put God's words into practice are labeled what?

_____

Where does the wise man build his house? _____

What happens when the rains come, the streams rise, and the winds blow?

_____

Those who hear and do not put God's words into practice are labeled what?

_____

Where does the foolish man build his house? _____

"Whoever can be trusted with very little can also be trusted with much, and whoever is dishonest with very little will also be dishonest with much. So if you have not been trustworthy in handling worldly wealth, who will trust you with true riches? And if you have not been trustworthy with someone else's property, who will give you property of your own?"

Luke 16:10–12 (NIV)

What happens when the rains come, the streams rise, and the winds blow?

_____

This parable is placed after the Sermon on the Mount which extends from Matthew 5:1—7:29.

📖 Look over this great sermon and read the Parable of the Wise and Foolish Builders in Matthew 7:24-29. Then answer this question:

What does it mean to hear and act on the words of Jesus?

_____

The sure foundation upon which we want to build this kingdom life is outlined in Jesus' sermon. The parable is thus a depiction of what happens when one uses the proper building materials and what happens to those who do not. Whether in the corporate world or in the church, when the storms come and we're put to the test, our focus on the things of the kingdom will give us a foundation from which to make wise, even shrewd, decisions.

I Have Decided

ANTIDOTE TO FEAR

I have a picture in my kitchen of an older man, possibly a monk, praying over his meal of bread and water. It is not a particularly beautiful picture, but it is a treasure to me because it was left to my sister and me by our grandmother. We commented one day during a visit that, like the man in the picture, we could see our grandfather praying over what little he had, whether it was food or possessions. I've heard of people who are left great fortunes, and I often wonder what that would be like. Then I realize many are left wondering what it would be like to have a possession that means so much because of the life lived by the person who owned it.

Our parable today begins with a question of inheritance posed to Jesus.

📖 Read Luke 12:13–21.

We don't know the issues the man with the inheritance question may have had with his brothers. All I know is these situations can be very tricky. Jesus must have sensed in the man's tone or manner that he had his own personal issues with money. So He tells this story—the Parable of the Rich Fool. At first glance, it appears the man has done nothing wrong. He is obviously a good farmer and through the sweat of his brow has managed a bumper crop. This isn't a fluke, because his barns are already full from the previous year's crop. He has managed his business well. So the man decides his next wise move is to build a bigger barn. Sounds reasonable. But then comes the hammer. That night the man's life will be over. He won't get to enjoy that fancy new barn or the fruit of his labor, to _"relax, eat, drink, be merry,"_ as he puts it.

Now before we judge this man self-righteously, let's consider our own barns and crops. By the world's standards, you and I have more than any one of us probably needs. When we meet with our financial advisors, we are told to save, save, save. Somehow we've translated that to horde, horde, horde.

So what could the man have done differently? He could have left some of the excess crop in the field for gleaners.

📖 Read Leviticus 19:9–10.

He could have provided for his family.

📖 Read Proverbs 13:22.

But what Jesus is addressing by answering the man's inheritance question with this parable is the thing at the heart of most money issues—fear and the placement of trust. When our security is found in accumulating enough, enough never seems to be enough. When we find our security in God, we no longer fear being without, because God is more than enough.

Where do you draw the line at "enough?" What is your measuring stick?

_____

_____

_____

In your calculations, do you consider the needs of others? Have you considered living on less so there is more to give away? Is fear or generosity more of a driver in your decisions?

📖 In the next parable, that of the Tower Builder and Warring King, another aspect of fear is addressed. Read Luke 14:25–32.

What is the fear of the tower builder?

_____

_____

What is the fear of the warring king?

_____

_____

Fear of failure and ridicule prevent a lot of people from doing what they are called to do. What fears keep you from trusting God? Mark the fears you struggle with the most in the list that follows.

- ☐ Fear of homelessness/hunger
- ☐ Fear of "losing it all"
- ☐ Fear of losing your job
- ☐ Fear of not having enough to last
- ☐ Fear of not providing for family
- ☐ Fear of bankruptcy
- ☐ Fear of not measuring up
- ☐ Fear of trying and failing
- ☐ Fear of dependency

When our security is found in accumulating enough, enough never seems to be enough. When we find our security in God, we no longer fear being without, because God is more than enough.

What does this parable teach is the antidote to fear?

_____

_____

Correctly estimating the cost will calm fears, ease anxiety, and properly place our focus. One thing is certain, either following Jesus or refusing to follow will cost one's all. Are you willing to give your all? When it comes to possessions, are you like the man in my grandfather's painting, grateful for what little you have, or you like the man with the barns, unable to truly enjoy what you have because you never seem to have enough?

I Have Decided

DAY FIVE

ALREADY AND NOT YET

I've never served in the military, but as I understand it, standing watch is one of the most important jobs. Watches are divided into shifts so the person standing watch is at his or her most alert. I have several friends who serve as firemen and policemen; both must be alert and ready to jump at a moment's notice when they are on watch.

The life of the Christian is characterized by a certain watchfulness. Here in Luke's Gospel, Jesus reminds His followers they are to be dressed and ready at a moment's notice.

We will look at the Parable of the Wise and Watchful in sections, as the story builds in urgency and risk in parts. Let's begin with Luke 12:35–40.

In this first scene, servants are awaiting the arrival of their master with lanterns burning. Jesus says that if the master finds his servants alert and attentive, his gratitude will result in an invitation to sit at the table of honor so *he* can serve *them*. The key is that like a thief coming in the night, the servants won't know when the master will return, so they must stay alert and ready. What do you think it means in a Christian's life to be dressed and ready?

_____

_____

Peter's question in verse 41 provides the introduction to the next section.

📖 Read Luke 12:42–46.

Jesus begins his answer with a question of his own. Record the first part of that question here.

_____

_____

_____

This time servants are awaiting the arrival of their master, and instead of remaining faithful and alert, one of the servants becomes impatient. Out of frustration and under the influence of alcohol, he turns on his fellow servants and beats them. When the manager suddenly returns, he rips the servant to shreds and casts him out.

📖 Jesus now summarizes His message. Read His summary in Luke 12:47–48.

What happens to the servant who knows his master's will but does not get ready or act on that knowledge? _____

What happens to the servant who does not know his master's will and yet does bad things? _____

Be careful not to read too much into this parable. It is not a parable about punishment or the validity of beating someone. The beatings are analogous to the suffering we will endure because of our own poor choices. If we don't know and choose to do what is wrong, and if we know and still choose the wrong path, we will suffer the consequences. However, for the one who is ignorant, God's grace will intervene. But woe to those of us who know better.

In summary, kingdom living is living with an eschatological, or end-of-times, long-range view. It requires constant watchfulness, alertness, and readiness. In what ways do you live in anticipation of Christ's return? In the areas of life listed below, write the ways you live in the present with an eye toward your eternal future. The first one is filled in as an example:

Physical care.
I take care of my body through diet and exercise because it is the temple of the living God and will one day will be transformed.

Spiritual care.

_____

_____

Family life.

_____

_____

Thought life.

_____

_____

Work.

_____

_____

Social life.

_____

_____

Kingdom living is living with an eschatological, or end-of-times, long-range view.

Hope doesn't deny the existence of trials, but instead hope allows us to live the "already" with a "not-yet" attitude.

Hope is the hallmark of this kind of living. Hope transforms our todays, giving perspective to our present trials. Hope doesn't deny the existence of trials, but instead hope allows us to live the "already" with a "not-yet" attitude. If you need hope today, look up these verses and write them out on index cards to remind you of the hope you now live in Jesus Christ.

Jeremiah 17:7–8
Lamentations 3:24–25
Romans 15:13
Psalm 25:4–5
Hebrews 11:1
Psalm 119:74
Isaiah 40:31

This is the reason we have hope—read 1 Thessalonians 4:14–18. After reading this, describe the hope it gives.

_____

_____

_____

_____

_____

Kingdom living is living in the present with the end in mind. As we've already said, it is an "already" and a "not-yet" way of life that anticipates the moment our Lord and master will return. Are you standing watch?

Discipleship the Jesus Way

PARABLES OF JESUS

LIVING INSIDE OUT

The concept of discipleship was not a New-Testament-Jesus invention. Discipling was an accepted student-teacher practice in the ancient world. For example, Aristotle was such a good disciple, or apprentice, of Plato that much of what we know of Plato's thoughts and ideas came to us through Aristotle. Although the Greek word (*mathetes*) translated *disciple* in the New Testament is not found in the Old Testament, the concept of a follower or adherent is. In the book of Second Kings, we learn of a guild, or school, of disciples in the service of Elisha. In Isaiah we read not only of his students but also of his desire to be a good student, or disciple, of God.

📖 Look up 2 Kings 2:3–7 and Isaiah 8:16; 50:4.

In these passages we begin to appreciate that discipleship was more than simply disseminating and receiving information. After reading the passages, how would you describe the relationship of disciple to teacher?

_____

_____

_____

A disciple was an imitator of his teacher, aligning his life and thoughts with that of his instructor. A disciple sought to mold his very way of life to that of his leader so he might inculcate his values, words, and actions. For this reason, Jesus chose twelve and said, "Come follow me." He wasn't looking for someone to simply record His words like a newspaper reporter on assignment. He was looking for imitators, disciples, who would follow His every move.

📖 Read 1 Corinthians 11:1 and Luke 6:40. When we are trained in the ways of Christ, what will we be?

_____

_____

Over the next several weeks, we will be looking at the parables loosely grouped under the heading of discipleship. These parables are about living a Christlike life, having a Christlike mind, and relating to the world in a Christlike way. This is kingdom living at its heart, the nitty-gritty how-to of Christian discipleship.

Let's begin by looking at a series of parables using one of Jesus' favorite images—that of a lamp.

📖 Read Matthew 5:14–16.

What do you think might be the relation between a light and a city?

_____

_____

What is the implied relation between good deeds and letting your light shine?

_____

_____

📖 Mark has a slightly different take on this parable in his Gospel. Read Mark 4:21–22.

How might a light on a stand disclose and reveal the hidden?

_____

_____

Because of its strategic location, a hilltop city provided refuge, protection, and security to a community. Like a lamp lit in a darkened room, the city on a hill was a beacon to all in the valley. All followers of Christ are to live as shining examples of love, compassion, and service so that those in the darkest places might see their light and be drawn to the source of that light. The word often rendered as *lights or lamp* in this passage is better translated as *luminaries*. The moon is a luminary, offering no light of its own. It can only reflect light from the sun. This passage makes it clear we can only reflect the light.

📖 Read John 12:35. Who is the light? _____

Here is a flip side to living in the light. When you and I live close to the light source, what was once hidden in the secrecy of darkness is revealed. All of us have secrets, secrets we keep from others and even those we keep from ourselves. Through the help of a counselor, I've opened dark closets and let the light penetrate those secrets. The light has disclosed long-held hurts,

All followers of Christ are to live as shining examples of love, compassion, and service so that those in the darkest places might see their light and be drawn to the source of that light.

faulty beliefs, and lies Satan has been using to hold me back. The darkness of these lies threatened to nearly overtake me, but in opening them to reflection and the warming rays of the Son, I was able to see what Satan was doing. God's light was able to reveal the truth of His love in my life. What secrets are you hiding because of fear?

_____

_____

_____

_____

Ask God to help you open those dark closets, and if He suggests it is time for a counselor, ask Him to help you find the right person with a lamp on a stand.

📖 Just prior to the Parable of the City on a Hill is its parallel, that of Salt. Read Matthew 5:13.

Until recently, salt was a curative. In southern Appalachia, meat was soaked in a salt bath or placed in salting boxes and then hung in smokehouses to complete the curing process. The salt prevented the spread of spoilage-causing bacteria in the meat. Beware when ordering a ham dinner in some parts of the South even today, because country-cured ham means salty ham, and I mean salty.

In some Bible translations we read salt can lose its *savor*, its distinctive taste or tang. I like this word, although it is not a word used too often today. Interestingly, when savorless salt is thrown out upon fields, it makes those fields barren. When you and I as followers of Christ lose our savor, we lose not only our curative properties in a world filled with corruption, but we may also have even the opposite effect. Instead of bringing life, we may actually prevent new life from forming.

Salt does its work from the inside, while light does its work on the outside. Being salt requires kingdom living in the midst of a contaminated world. We can't hide in the safety of our churches and among our Christian friends and be salty. Eventually, we'll lose our saltiness. What steps can you take this week to live a salty life?

_____

_____

_____

Finally, being a luminary requires two things: being in a position to receive light from the source, and living from the inside out. Reflection is our inner light shining through our outer lives—in the deeds we do. What deeds will you do this week to reflect the light in you?

_____

_____

_____

Being a luminary requires two things: being in a position to receive light from the source, and living from the inside out.

KNOWING GOOD FRUIT

When we moved into our present house, my husband and I were excited about the mature orange tree the previous owners had planted. For months our mouths watered as we imagined the juice dripping down our arms from the sweet orange flesh. When the time came for harvest, we borrowed a juicer from my aunt and ceremoniously picked our first fruit. We nearly choked when we bit into it, for it was sour and dry—nothing like the fruit from the trees in the backyard of my childhood home down South. We later learned it would take several years of faithful fertilizing and pruning at just the right intervals to produce the sweet fruit we longed for.

The idea of good and bad fruit, good and bad trees, was a common one for Jesus. That may be because it paints a picture any of us can understand, especially anyone who's tried to get good fruit from a tree.

📖 Read the Parable of the Thorns and Thistles in Matthew 7:15–20.

The sheep reference easily leads from the two previous verses, where Jesus speaks of the narrow gate. One would have understood the connection to a gate in the sheepfold leading to good pasture. At night a shepherd could not use his eyes to see, especially on a moonless night. Instead he felt his sheep as they passed through the gate. He would have recognized an imposter, even one so cunning as to put on *"sheep's clothing."*

There are many who profess faith in God, many who talk a good talk. So how are we to know when we have the real deal? First, let me caution—this is easier said than done. Jesus says we will know them by their fruit, but just what is this fruit? Let's back up one more verse to see.

What is Matthew 7:12 known as in Christian circles?

_____

The Golden Rule is the fertilizer for good fruit. We will know if someone is the real deal if they practice the Golden Rule. However, society has warped this rule a little. It doesn't say, "Do to others *as they do to you*" but *"as you would have them do to you."* If we want honesty in our business dealings, we need to fertilize with honesty; if we want compassion when we are hurting, we need to fertilize with compassion; and if we want patience, kindness, and understanding from our family and friends, we need to fertilize with those. When we fertilize our own lives, God does an amazing thing. He not only produces good fruit from our own trees, He produces that fruit in others.

Sounds simple. But it is much harder to do.

It is easy to do to others as I want them to do to me when that person is sweet and deserving. It is easy when there is no financial gain for doing otherwise. It is easy when it won't cost me. But when following the Golden Rule requires eating humble pie, or simply if the person in question rubs me the wrong way, then doing to others as I want them to do to me—and as Christ has done for me—becomes an intentional act. This is obedience. When all else screams for me to act otherwise and I still choose to do as I should, this is fruit-producing righteousness.

What makes it difficult for you to follow the Golden Rule? Is it how others act, or is it more a question of what it will cost you?

_____

_____

_____

This first reference to fruit in Matthew puts the focus on outside actions, but the next helps us to see that good fruit is an inside-out job.

📖 Read Matthew 12:33–35.

The Pharisees had just accused Jesus of being in league with Satan, after He cast demons out of a blind and deaf man. As we read His words, we can see Jesus is angry. "You can't have it both ways," He says. Either the tree and fruit are good or the tree and fruit are bad. There is no such thing as good fruit on a bad tree, or bad fruit on a good tree. Then once again we find that wonderful little word *for*. What tumbles out of the mouth is what bubbles up from the depths of the heart. Plain and simple; if evil is in the heart, evil will flow from the mouth.

With the first parable we understand that bearing good fruit is about how we treat others, and with this parable we see that bearing good fruit is about the kind of treasure in our hearts, whether good or bad.

I wish I could say good things always came out of my mouth. But that is not the case. Whenever harsh, impatient, judgmental, or unlovely things escape my lips, I'm reminded of this Scripture. Yes, I have Jesus in my heart, but in those instances I'm not bearing good fruit. I'm not saying (and neither is Jesus) that if I utter bad things, I am a bad person. This parable is about fruit and how we can tell if someone is trustworthy. When bad things slip from my mouth, my fruit is demonstrating I need some God time. In these times I'd have to say I'm not very trustworthy because my treasure is focused on earthly, human things and not God things.

If poor verbal fruit is harming your witness, ask God to reveal the treasure buried within your heart that needs removal. Record your thoughts here.

_____

_____

_____

_____

_____

Now ask God to help you replace that evil treasure with godly treasure.

What tumbles out of the mouth is what bubbles up from the depths of the heart.

A LOVE-HATE RELATIONSHIP

More volumes have been written and more sermons preached about this parable than any other. Those with little or no faith have used this story in their speeches and books. It has inspired paintings, sculptures, poetry, and films. Even our language has been influenced by it in that the phrase "good Samaritan" has come to mean someone who helps a stranger. The Parable of the Good Samaritan has been used to illustrate such diverse themes as compassion, ethics, and race relations. While all of these themes are there, and while this parable speaks to us on multiple levels as evidenced by its popularity, as good students of the Bible we must set aside all that we've heard. Our task is to discern what was intended by Jesus and by the Gospel writer, Luke, in the telling of this story.

We begin with the context of the parable, which Luke provides us.

📖 Read it in Luke 10:25–28 and fill in the table.

Round One. The lawyer stands to test Jesus.

The lawyer's first question	
Jesus' question	
The lawyer's answer	
Jesus' answer	

Round Two. The lawyer seeks to justify himself.

The lawyer's second question	
Jesus' question	
The lawyer's answer	
Jesus' answer	

Unlike civil or constitutional lawyers of today, lawyers of Jesus' day were defenders of the law of Moses, more akin to a combination professor of biblical studies and a bishop. Like today's lawyers, these men were known for their verbal acumen and sharp intellect. When this lawyer *"stood up to test Jesus,"* this would have been high drama, better than any courtroom drama we've ever witnessed.

Demonstrating his verbal skill, the lawyer asked a tricky question. On the surface it appears innocuous: "How can I get to heaven?" If that is what he meant, then Jesus' response doesn't make sense. The key in understanding the lawyer's question is the word *inherit*. In Mosaic law, inheritance and obedience to the Torah were eternally linked to the promised kingdom of God. In using this coded language, the lawyer was asking, "So what kind of kingdom are you setting up?" He wanted to know if the kingdom Jesus was preaching was in line with what he knew.

This was the man's first problem, and it is one with which I'm quite familiar. Often I approach the Word of God with what I believe, what I've been taught, what I know. When I place what I believe, have been taught, and know in front of what God wants to say, I've prejudiced that Word and might miss God's actual words.

Jesus recognizes the man's handicap and uses a familiar lawyer-like move. He turns the table and asks the lawyer a question: *"How do you read the law?"* The lawyer wisely responds with quotations from two Torah heavyweights.

📖 Deuteronomy 6:5. How are we to love God?

_____

_____

📖 Leviticus 19:18. How are enemies and neighbors linked in this passage?

_____

_____

It is funny that when we are dealing with Jesus, some things just slip out of our mouths. Truths we don't even know. I picture Jesus smiling, and the man squirming. "You said it." Jesus says. "Now go and do it." The lawyer's been routed by his own words. When I've been found outed before God, I have a choice: surrender or defend. The lawyer isn't at the surrender stage yet, so he seeks to defend himself by asking what he thinks is a clever question: "Who is my neighbor?" But Jesus cannot be outwitted. He responds with the Parable of the Good Samaritan.

📖 Read it in Luke 10:30–37.

How does the parable address the lawyer's question (both the spoken one and the unspoken)?

_____

_____

_____

Until I did the work on the context of this parable, which we went through above, I'd missed the emphasis on enemies and neighbors in the parable. The victim of bandits and the two passersby were Jewish, but the only one who came to the man's aid was a Samaritan. As they were considered half-breeds—part Jewish and part Gentile—Samaritans were hated by full-blooded Jews. Imagine the outrage when the hero of Jesus' story is a hated Samaritan. To drive that stake in deeper, the Samaritan didn't just stop and

When I place what I believe, have been taught, and know in front of what God wants to say, I've prejudiced that Word and might miss God's actual words.

Did You Know?
THE SAMARITANS

Samaritans, even today, consider themselves to be the descendants of the ancient Joseph tribes of Ephraim and Manasseh and the levitical priests who have lived in Shechem (Nablus) since the Israelite conquest of Canaan. They remain true to historic Mosaic faith, however, they view Judaism as an Israelite heresy derived from the schism from the priest Eli when he established a rival sanctuary at Shiloh.

hold the man's head or call for help. List all the things the Samaritan did for the injured Jewish man.

_____

_____

_____

As Jesus went on and on, listing step after step the Samaritan took to help the Jew, the lawyer must have been thinking, *Enough already!* He couldn't imagine doing for a Samaritan what this Samaritan did for the Jew. But he had to admit, when Jesus asked him the question, that the one who was a neighbor to the injured man was *"the one who showed him mercy."* His hatred of the Samaritans so strong he couldn't bring himself to say the word.

Who brings you that same reaction? What about terrorists who saw off the heads of innocents? What about child molesters or rapists? Are there individuals that just the mention of their name gives you a visceral reaction?

List them here.

_____

_____

_____

The Bible calls these people enemies. It doesn't deny that we'll have enemies, but the parable makes it clear we are to love them as neighbors. We aren't asked to treat them as family, just neighbors—neighbors whom we take pity on and whom we serve with concrete steps of compassion. Imagine what this kingdom would look like if all believers treated their enemies this way. Imagine if you treated your enemies this way. Jesus doesn't say we must love what these people do; we can still hate that. No, we are to love the people God created. What are a few concrete steps you could take to love your enemies?

_____

_____

_____

Discipleship the Jesus Way

DAY FOUR

ON GOD'S PAYROLL

A gain, our parables today can be taken differently if not read within their context. The context this time is a warning to maintain a forgiving attitude when faced with opposition, even opposition from within the ranks. Jesus tells His followers they must be ready to forgive someone *"seven times a day"* if need be. One of the disciples shouted from the crowd, "Increase our faith!"

📖 Read the first part of this parable pair in Luke 17:5–6.

What is the point of this parable in light of the context?

_____

_____

This is called the Parable of the Mulberry Tree so as not to confuse it with the Parable of the Mustard Seed. Jesus knew that in order to have what it takes to repeatedly offer forgiveness when a brother or sister wounds, the disciples would need a deeper faith. This wasn't a matter of quantity but of quality. They needed deeper, not more, faith.

📖 Swiftly Jesus moves into the second parable. Read it in Luke 17:7–10.

The slave, or servant, has been toiling all day. When he comes home, all he wants is to sit down and eat, but his master is ready for his meal and demands to eat. So the dutiful servant puts on his apron and, bone-tired but dutiful, prepares the meal,.

Now, I can hear every working woman out there saying, "Preach it, brother!" How many of us come home to a hungry family after we've worked a 9-to-5 job or completed a mile-long to-do list in between serving as mom's taxi service? "When's dinner?" everyone whines as you are still unloading groceries from the car and letting the dog out to do his business.

What comes next in this parable is tough medicine for us superwomen. Verse 9 says, *"Do you thank the slave for doing what was commanded?"* We want to shout, "Well, yes we do, if we are polite!" But that is not the point of this parable. This is not a parable about the master. This is not a picture of God and how He views or treats us. That would be taking the parable out of context. In context, this parable is about our attitude. When we work for God, are we expecting a gold star or pat on the back for doing our job? The question is, Why do we do what we do? If our expectation is recognition or reward, then our expectation is misplaced. It's not that we won't be recognized or rewarded, because God promises that elsewhere in Scripture, but it is the expectation that sours our countenance.

Having worked both as a full-time church staff member and as a volunteer member of the laity, I'm always troubled when we commission mission teams. What kind of message are we sending when we say, "These people and these people only are doing something worthy of God's extra blessing?" By not commissioning the teacher, the mom, the office worker, or truck driver, are we not saying that what they are doing is less godly, less a ministry?

This parable makes it clear that God sees not only what we do and why we do it but also how we do it. In this first parable, working in God's vineyard is akin to serving His kingdom purposes.

📖 Read Matthew 21:28–32.

What did Jesus say John the Baptist was showing them?

_____

_____

What do you think this means?

_____

_____

The ways of righteousness are the ways of the kingdom. Said another way, kingdom ways lead to righteousness. When you and I choose to obey and work in God's vineyard, wherever that may be, we are walking in the ways of righteousness. Whether that is working at the church, going on a mission

When we work for God, are we expecting a gold star or pat on the back for doing our job? The question is, Why do we do what we do? If our expectation is recognition or reward, then our expectation is misplaced.

trip, or simply doing our 9-to-5 jobs, we are working for Him if we are doing our tasks with an eye toward pleasing our master and Lord.

List the jobs and roles you play on a weekly basis.

_____

_____

_____

Now place a checkmark next to those tasks where you feel you do a good job of doing them "unto the Lord." Circle those in which a little reorientation is in order. The next time you step into these roles, ask God to help you fulfill your job as His employee.

GLITTER AND GOLD

The two parables we will look at today are not the parables I'd share with brand-new Christians excited about their new faith. Just as we don't want to put an excited and anxious expectant mom at the dinner table next to the worried and brokenhearted mom of a troubled teen, these two parables are only for the mature. Not that they aren't true, but they are tough.

The first one comes after a day filled with miracles. Read Matthew 8:14–22. Jesus had just healed Peter's mother-in-law, and when word spread, people brought all the sick to the house. Jesus spent the rest of the day casting out demons and curing all who were ill. The yard must have looked like a triage center, except here everyone was healed. Caught up in the excitement and drama, a scribe burst out, *"Teacher, I will follow you wherever you go."*

Hollywood sells us on the glamorous lifestyle of the rich and famous. When the lights flash and mobs of people push for autographs, it appears the stars have it all. But, we've also seen behind the scenes. Celebrity life is not all it's built up to be. It is a lonely and often empty life. When the scribe blurts out his enamored confession, Jesus realizes the man is just caught up in the moment. So He points out that if the man does decide to follow Him, he too could be homeless. Now, not everyone who follows Jesus will be homeless, but the point is, it's not all glitz and glamour.

The second part of this parable is a little more difficult. A second follower comes to Jesus and says he's in too: "Just let me go bury my father first." Jesus responds with some tough medicine. "Let the dead bury the dead. You follow me." Wow! Could Jesus really be that callous? Some scholars have pointed out that if the man's father were already dead, then he wouldn't have been at Peter's house listening to Jesus. Two options are more likely: first, the man's father was gravely ill and expected to die, so the man was asking to delay following Jesus to be with his aging father. The second option (and the one I prefer) is that the man was doing what many of us do when God calls us to something that seems difficult. We make excuses. We'll say, "I'm happy to say yes to that, but let me take care of this first."

What is God asking you to do that you've been offering excuses about?

_____

_____

_____

📖 Although this next parable does not follow the previous one, it does follow the same theme. Read Matthew 10:32–38.

If there is anywhere it is hardest to live out our faith, it is within our own families. Family members know most, if not all, of our secrets. They know who we are unvarnished. This makes it difficult to live a holy and sanctified life before them. Likewise, we know who they are, and all of their secrets, which makes it difficult to love them as Jesus asks us to. Those of us who've sought to witness to our families know just how divisive that can be.

How ironic that at His birth Jesus was heralded as the Prince of Peace, and yet the very mention of His name to some is like a sword, dividing loved ones. This parable is not negating that promise of peace; the point of this parable is something different. The point is summarized in verses 37–38. Summarize that point in your own words here.

_____

_____

_____

The kingdom of God is not all gold and glitter. It requires some tough choices. All that sparkles is not glitter and gold. If you choose to follow God, you may not have a home or friends or success as the world defines it. You can't control things in God's kingdom, and therefore you may have to set aside your excuses in order to do what is being asked of you.

Finally, where it really counts—in our families—living a kingdom life might cause division. It may even cost you your dearest relationships. Because if they push back and don't wish to join you in following God, God requires a choice. Those who've made that painful choice know they've certainly taken up their cross to follow Jesus.

List the unsaved or unrepentant family members you are praying for today.

_____

_____

_____

_____

🙏 If you've been at odds with family because of your faith, ask God to help you remain faithful. Express your desire that it not come to a choice between Him and family, but that if it does, your heart remains with Him.

"Anyone who loves their father or mother more than me is not worthy of me; anyone who loves their son or daughter more than me is not worthy of me. Whoever does not take up their cross and follow me is not worthy of me."

Matthew 10:37–38 (NIV)

Notes

Discipleship Part Two

PARABLES OF JESUS

Discipleship
Part Two

DAY ONE

THE POINT

Just like most of our modern-day preachers, when it comes to images and parabolic metaphors, Jesus had His favorites. He returned to several themes over and over again, but with different intentions or points to make. This causes some confusion for us today. That being said, we must guard against mixing the different narratives in our minds and thus missing the meaning in each. Such is the case with the parable before us. It is called the Parable of the Grain of Mustard Seed as opposed to the mustard seed parable we studied earlier. As you read it, think about these questions:

Why did Jesus use this metaphor here (context)? What was His purpose in using it again?

📖 Read Matthew 17:19–20.

The scene for this parable is significant. A father brings his epileptic son to Jesus because the disciples were unable to cure him. Jesus cures the boy and when the disciples ask why they had been unable to do the same, Jesus tells them this parable.

I find it a little odd that Jesus tells these men their faith was not as big as a grain of mustard seed. Don't you? After all, they had enough faith to follow Jesus and to go cast out demons in His name. That takes huge faith, doesn't it? It is of note that this parable wasn't told to the crowds; it was shared with the faithful. Jesus wasn't saying these men had no faith. They did. But there is a depth of faith required if you and I are to do great things in the name of

Jesus. It is the faith symbolized in the tiny mustard seed, which is planted in the depths of the ground. No one, by looking at the seed, would think this insignificant kernel could become anything. But deep in the DNA of that seed is the vision of the tree it might become. It "believes" it can become that tree and acts in accordance with that belief. It doesn't become the tree on its own, only God can do that. But without the actions of putting down roots and sprouting, all actions tied to the belief, it could not do what it believed. The disciples had done the right things, but deep in their hearts they didn't quite believe they could do it. Jesus reminds us with this parable that all we need is a tiny bit of this deep-held faith—mustard-seed faith—and we can move mountains.

Describe mustard-seed faith in your own words.

_____

_____

_____

_____

Another favorite metaphor of Jesus is that of sheep. We've already looked at Jesus as the Great Shepherd. We also looked at you and me as the sheep of His pasture, entering through Jesus the gate. This time the analogy follows two incidents of Jesus' breaking Sabbath laws. Skim Matthew 12:1–8 and answer these questions:

What is Jesus doing that has the Pharisees so upset?

_____

_____

_____

Fill in the blanks to Jesus' answer from verse 7:
I desire _____ and not _____.

In the second incident in Matthew 12:9–10, Jesus deals a double blow to the religious leaders. He heals a withered hand *in the* synagogue *on the* Sabbath. When the Pharisees try to corner Him, Jesus once again uses His familiar metaphor of the sheep.

Read Matthew 12:11–12.

In this Parable of the Sheep in the Pit, Jesus artfully reveals the Pharisees' hypocrisy. They would certainly rescue a sheep of their own, even if it were the Sabbath. However, we miss the deeper meaning if we do not tie this to the quote from Hosea 6:6 quoted earlier in verse 7.

Read this passage in Hosea. What do you think Jesus was saying to the Pharisees by using this quote and tying it to the parable?

_____

_____

_____

_____

In a masterful way Jesus was pointing out that although the Pharisees were faithful with their temple sacrifices, they had missed the mark. Acts of love, not ritual sacrifice, were the things that demonstrated knowledge of God. Nevertheless, in the first Sabbath-breaking incident, they were upset because Jesus and His disciples were plucking wheat on the Sabbath. In the second, Jesus was healing on the Sabbath. Their focus was on the Mosaic law, but they were completely missing the point of the law, which was to demonstrate love to God (and Jesus's actions show that to demonstrate love to God we show love to others). In God's kingdom it is always people above principle. That is the point.

DOGS AND LOGS

Sometimes a little understanding of the geography of a parable's setting helps us to understand the meaning. Jesus has been in Gennesaret, known as the paradise of Galilee. Our parable picks up as Jesus is leaving this garden district in the Holy Land to go to Tyre, a Gentile city in present-day Lebanon. No explanation is given as to why Jesus makes this move. The mission to the Gentiles has not been announced. Nevertheless, we are told that along the way a Canaanite woman begins shouting. Canaanites were Syro-Phoenicans, natives of the land the Israelites conquered centuries earlier. Canaanites were known to worship Ashtoreth, the queen of heaven, and were therefore idolaters and consequently hated and shunned by Jews.

📖 Read Matthew 15:21–28.

We can presume because of the way the story was set up that this woman had appealed to her god to no avail. When she did not get the aid she sought from her own god, she sought out the Son of David. By calling Him "Son of David," she was professing Him to be Israel's Messiah, the seed of David (Luke 1:31). By referencing Jesus as Lord, the woman acknowledged Jesus' deity, dominion, and power.

Most puzzling is Jesus' response. He ignores her. When the disciples ask Him to send her away, He replies with a parable illustration. Record His words from verse 24 here.

_____

_____

After she kneels before him and begs, Jesus replies with a second parable illustration, in verse 26. Record it here.

_____

_____

Dog was a common racial slur. Why would Jesus say this? We first must recognize that it was Jesus who chose to go into the community of dogs. There is no other reason given for His travel there except her. Following this episode, Jesus and the disciples are back in Galilee, so we must assume His purpose for being in Tyre is this woman's need. So why did He call her a dog?

Sometimes it is easier to recognize our own bad behavior when someone else does what we've dismissed in our lives. The Scripture doesn't say this, but there must have been some nonverbal communication between Jesus and the woman. Because she didn't take Jesus' words as an insult, but accepted the slur, I imagine she looked into His eyes and saw acceptance and love. She was willing to be called whatever this man wanted to call her because she trusted Him. *"Even the dogs eat the crumbs that fall from their masters' table,"* she says to Him. Record Jesus' answer in verse 28.

_____

_____

_____

📖 Earlier in Matthew we encounter another reference to dogs. Read Matthew 7:6.

The wild dogs Jesus is speaking of are more akin to savage wolves. Swine were considered unclean animals under Mosaic law. Thus, we are to be discriminate with the things of God. Savage wolves and unclean swine cannot appreciate the pearls of the kingdom. They will trample them and then turn on those who represent the truth.

The preamble to this parable contains two more figures of speech that when combined with the two we just examined offer thoughts on a single theme—that of judgment.

📖 Read Matthew 7:1–5. Record the admonition in verse 1.

_____

_____

Did You Know?

PERCEPTIONS OF CHRISTIANS

In a recent Barna survey the most common perceptions cited by non-Christians about Christians is we are judgmental (87%), hypocritical (85%), old-fashioned (78%), and too involved in politics (75%). The Barna Group, Ltd, 2009.

The simplicity of this parable can lull us into taking it too casually. But the images of a man with a log sticking out of his eye pointing at the splinter in another's eye is a striking picture of self-righteousness. Sadly, the descriptive most often used today by non-Christians to describe Christians is *judgmental*. I'm ashamed to say that at times I major in faultfinding. It is so easy for me to see the faults in others while ignoring my own. Do you have a faultfinding problem? You may want to try this trick someone taught me. When my finger begins to wag accusingly at others, I imagine a large log dangling from my eye. It is not a pretty picture. However, if you give it a try, don't be surprised when you see how quickly your pointed finger becomes a helping hand.

When this parable is combined with the Parable of the Dogs and Swine, we get a clear picture of the danger of unwise judgment and the need for wise judgment. Hypocrisy defines the first type of judgment, and discernment is the nature of the second.

WOE IS I

Often left out of discussions is a set of parables found in Matthew 23. This hard-hitting narrative delivers tough medicine. Let's begin the study of this important chapter by looking at what has just occurred.

📖 Skim Matthew 22:41–46. Jesus just asked the Pharisees a question they could not answer. From verse 46 summarize the end result of this confrontation.

_____

_____

📖 The Pharisees have been silenced. With this in mind, begin reading Matthew 23:1–4 and answer the following questions:

What were the crowds supposed to do concerning the Pharisees' teaching?

_____

_____

Therefore, was the teaching good? _____

Then what was the problem Jesus had with the Pharisees?

_____

_____

As we will see in the rest of this chapter, the main issue Jesus had with the Pharisees was not their theology but the practice of those beliefs. We can believe all the right things but still be on the wrong side of Jesus. In verse 4 what is Jesus comparing the Pharisees to?

_____

_____

The image is of a pack animal so heavily burdened that the animal can barely stand. The Pharisees burdened the people with so many rules and regulations and then doesn't lift a hand to lighten their load. How did they do this?

📖 Let's read further, verses 5–7.

Two pieces of information will help us understand this parable. First, phylacteries were little boxes tied to the forehead and wrists containing verses from the Torah. Second, there were five double knots on each fringe of a rabbi's prayer shawl, making a total of ten knots, representing the Ten Commandments. These were visual reminders of the inner change that was to have taken place when following the law, but for the Pharisees it was all an outside job. How did the actions described in these verses add to the burdens the people were bearing?

_____

_____

We can believe all the right things but still be on the wrong side of Jesus.

_____

_____

What do we do today that can similarly add to the burdens people feel?

_____

_____

_____

Many people feel that Christians have it all together, that we never struggle with the same things they struggle with. They look at us on the outside and never know the doubt, the shame, or the pain we hold inside. When we become real before others instead of hiding behind a Christian mask, we strip away one of Satan's tools. We actually begin to unburden others.

The next part of this chapter is often called the eight woes that Jesus pronounces against those who refuse to remove their mask of hypocrisy. This is tough stuff.

📖 If you have the courage, read the first three woes, in Matthew 23:13–22.

The first two woe statements are a continuation of the theme of the previous section. The Pharisees were not practicing what they preached and therefore were not leading people to God but away from Him. In the third woe statement, Jesus switches from the stinging label _hypocrites_ to the even more outrageous _blind guides_. What do you think the point is of this third warning?

_____

_____

_____

All of God's words are applicable to each of us every day and in every way.

These teachers of Torah have been bound by the oath they took to love God with their whole hearts, minds, and souls. However, when they found it convenient, they sidestepped the rules and said, "Well, God didn't really mean . . ." They were blinded by their own self-interest. More importantly, they were blind and leading others right off a cliff. When you and I justify that only some of God's words apply to us, we are just like the Pharisees, blinded by our own self-centeredness. All of God's words are applicable to each of us every day and in every way.

📖 Read the next woe statement in verses 23–24, containing two parable illustrations.

In the first parable Jesus is comparing the giving of _____, _____, and _____ to the harder practice of giving _____, _____, and _____. It was easy and a matter of pride for the Pharisees to tithe from their abundance of spices, but much more costly for them to give justice, mercy, and faith.

In the second Jesus is comparing the straining of a _____ to the swallowing of a _____. The pious used cheesecloth to strain their tea so they would not unknowingly swallow an unclean bug, which would in turn make them impure. Of course, it is hyperbole to suggest anyone could swallow a camel, but that is exactly what the Pharisees were doing. A steady diet of pride makes anyone impure.

Do you have a pride problem? If you do, picture yourself piously straining the brew of self-centerdness you sip on with the result being a camel in your cup. What we think of as a small issue is really a big sin in God's eye.

MASQUERADE

The fifth woe statement contains a wonderful parable picture. Read verses 25–26. What is Jesus saying with this parable?

_____

_____

_____

We may look good on the outside, but when the inside is dirty with an all-about-me-grime, we are unclean. Simply saying all the right things and doing the right things when we are with our church friends doesn't cut it with God. He's looking for a clean plate and cup, both inside and out.

Lest we think we've done a good job by just cleaning the dishes, Luke warns us with these words from Jesus.

📖 Read Luke 11:24–26. What else do we need to do?

_____

_____

_____

We must begin with a clean house, but that is only a first step. A clean house is an invitation for guests. If we do not fill our homes with love, kindness, peace, and joy, the uninvited guests of bitterness, strife, and all that is unlovely will make our clean homes dirty once again. Satan's minions are ready to move into a heart not already occupied with the goodness of the Lord. In the list that follows, mark those things that fill your heart (your home).

❏ Love
❏ **Impatience**
❏ Joy
❏ **Judgment**
❏ **Pessimism**
❏ Contentment
❏ Peace
❏ **Strife**
❏ **Bitterness**
❏ Kindness
❏ **Jealousy**
❏ Harmony

If we do not fill our homes with love, kindness, peace, and joy, the uninvited guests of bitterness, strife, and all that is unlovely will make our clean homes dirty once again.

If you marked more of the boldface items, ask God to give you more of His goodness (those things not boldface in the list) so there will be no room for Satan's uninvited guests.

One more thought: most of us don't have the luxury of cleaning our house once and expecting it to stay that way for very long. Our spiritual homes are the same. They require daily attention, daily cleaning, and daily refilling with the good things of Christ. Otherwise, we will end up with uninvited guests that may become difficult to send packing.

Some people have a picture of Jesus as always sweet and never uttering a cross word, but it is difficult to read this highly charged narrative without feeling His grief, anger, and even hatred at what Satan had wrought through those who were called to be God's. If we dare, these words of warning are here for us too. These last two woes contain some of Jesus' most memorable parabolic illustrations, spoken to help us stay the course to which we were called.

📖 Read Matthew 23:27–28. What is Jesus comparing in this first illustration?

_____

_____

You and I can only be full of life or death. There is no in-between.

What a gruesome image! Once a year the sepulchers were whitewashed to make them appear more attractive. Yet this could not hide the fact that they contained decaying and often diseased bodies. Unlike cemetaries today where bodies have been embalmed, the bodies in these cemeteries were simply rotting, diseases and all. Just being near these tombs meant breathing in the contaminated air. Jesus was saying the Pharisees were like whitewashed tombstones, appearing fresh and clean but full of dead men's bones. You and I can only be full of life or death. There is no in-between.

The eighth and final woe is a summary or continuation of this last illustration. It continues the tomb picture, but is a stinging blow to the Pharisees' pride. Jesus is calling them out. They have nowhere to hide.

📖 Read verses 29–36.

Many of the prophets and priests whose tombs the Pharisees pretended to decorate and honor had been murdered at the hands of the Pharisees themselves or by their ancestors. As if reading their minds, Jesus says they cannot claim, "Well, I would not have done that had I been there with my ancestors." For they had not changed their ways, and Jesus hints that soon, like the prophets of old, He himself will be flogged and murdered at their hands, and for this they will be condemned to hell.

📖 In Genesis it is unclear why Abel's gift is deemed acceptable and Cain's is not, but read Hebrews 11:4. What made Abel righteous?

_____

_____

📖 Now read about Zechariah, son of Barachiah, in 2 Chronicles 24:20–22.

Second Chronicles is the last book of the Jewish canon, the books they consider to be in their bible, therefore, Zechariah would have been the last righteous person murdered, with Able being the first. Woe indeed to the Pharisees as the blood of all of the righteous from Abel's day to Zechariah's was poured upon them for their part in Jesus' death.

But let's not get too haughty and say the same thing the Pharisees said to Jesus, "Well, I would not have done that had I been there." When you and I fail to walk the talk, when we preach what we do not practice, we are joining the league of Pharisees that have lived through the ages. Only when we remove the masks that blind us to what we are doing, only when we become honest with others and ourselves, only then will we become the disciples of Jesus Christ we are meant to be.

If you have been living behind a mask, take time today to bow before God and in an act of bravery, remove that mask. Write your prayer of repentance in the space below and then stand up to live boldly and mask free.

_____

_____

_____

_____

_____

DANGER AHEAD!

One of the harshest charges anyone can lay against another is that of treason. Treason is so heinous a crime because a person who was trusted used that position to turn on his or her own country. One day when Jesus was performing yet more miracles, tthe religious leaders accused Jesus of the unthinkable.

📖 Read the Parable of the Strong Man in Mark 3:22–27.

How does tying up the strong man relate to the miracle of casting out demons?

_____

_____

_____

Simply put, Jesus could not have been in cahoots with Satan while at the same time casting off Satan's efforts. That would be nonsensical. Jesus was not treasonous. He came to bind Satan, not assist him. Only after binding him could Jesus display the glory of the Father. If you and I are bound, caught up in addictions and afflictions, we must first tie up the strong man by casting lies and falsehoods aside. We do this by believing Jesus can be trusted with our secrets, our faults, and our sins. He is on our side. He is loyal. He uses truth to tie Satan up and to set you and me free. Only as free people can we fully display the Father's glory.

What lies is Satan using to bind you?

_____

_____

_____

_____

"But Cheri," I'm sometimes asked, "aren't you afraid to take those steps into the unknown?" My honest answer is, "Yes, I am, but the more I take them, the more confident I become that my unknowing is His knowing."

The biggest lie Satan still uses is the one that says Jesus is working against you, that He could never forgive you. But you have been created in God's image, and He claims you as one of His own (although one may have yet to acknowledge his or her place in the kingdom, Scripture makes it clear that God has staked His claim). To work against you would be treasonous, and Jesus is not treasonous. He loves you! He is loyal to you and is ready and willing to bind Satan in your life—if only you will ask.

If you have ever been worn out fighting with yourself. then you know another way that Satan binds people. You know what I'm talking about— when you think so strongly one way one minute and then the next you are arguing the opposing view. After a full day of this, you feel as though you've been to a boxing match where you are the punching bag. It's exhausting! This is a house divided against itself, and this house will not stand. That is Satan's goal. He wants to bring down your house. But Jesus is the support beam for a divided house. He can tie up those warring thoughts and discordant views and in their place He will bring peace and harmony.

📖 Two more ploys of Satan are expressed in this next parable. Read the Parable of the Yeast in Matthew 16:6–12 and answer these questions:

What were the disciples' focused on? _____

When Jesus referred to the yeast of the Pharisees, what was He referencing?

_____

_____

The Pharisees were legalists, and their demands were spiritually deadening. The Sadducees were rationalists; they did not believe in things that could not be explained naturally. The disciples were missing what Jesus was saying because they were focused on the things they could see with their eyes and control with their wills. Satan desires nothing more than to keep our hearts and minds captive to the rational, the explainable, and the controllable. These were the teaching tools of the Pharisees and Sadducees, and the disciples were following that teaching.

"Beware the yeast," Jesus says. These are false teachings, ploys of Satan. One cannot live in the Spirit and at the same time in Satan's playground. If your mind immediately goes to the rational and explainable, and if you are only comfortable with what is controllable and knowable, ask God to give you a willingness to take the "unleavened" path.

"But Cheri," I'm sometimes asked, "aren't you afraid to take those steps into the unknown?"

My honest answer is, "Yes, I am, but the more I take them, the more confident I become that my unknowing is His knowing."

Write the words to Luke 10:3 here.

_____

_____

We are sent where danger lurks. God doesn't need lightbulbs in the daylight. He doesn't need salt in the sea. Instead, He sends us where He needs us. He needs sweet lambs among wolves, springs of water in dry lands, and bread in empty bowls. Where are you serving as …
a lamb among wolves? _____
a spring of water in a dry land? _____
bread in an empty bowl? _____

It could be the office where you work, a club or fitness center to which you belong, your child's school or PTA, a civic group, a political group, your own neighborhood, or even your own family. Being a follower of Christ is sometimes dangerous. But God has promised us He is aware of our every move. He is with us, and in fact, he knows when a single hair falls from our heads.

📖 For assurance, read Matthew 10:29–31.

I remember my father singing the old hymn "His Eye Is on the Sparrow," based upon this parable. The last words of that great hymn repeat the promise that because God's eye is on the sparrow, "I know He watches me." To personalize this parable's promise, complete the paraphrase below, filling in your name where applicable.

Are not two sparrows sold for a penny? Yet not one of them will fall to the ground apart from the will of _____ Father. And even the very hairs of _____ head are all numbered. So don't be afraid; I, _____, am worth more than many sparrows.

> *God doesn't need lightbulbs in the daylight. He doesn't need salt in the sea.*

Notes

Discipleship Part Three

PARABLES OF JESUS

HUMBLE PIE

If you were to boil the concept of the kingdom of God down to one word, what would that be? Circle your one word or write it in the space below.

Life	Joy	Peace	Surrender
Freedom	Sacrifice	Service	Contentment
Love	Humility	Prayer	Liberty
Spirit-led	Christlikeness	Assurance	Power
Forgiveness	Other _____		

Jesus said that the law and all the words of the prophets are summed in the word *love*. But *love* is a tricky word; it has many different meanings. In the list above, I would not have initially circled the word *humility*. Yet that is one facet of the kind of love that represents the kingdom of God. Just as all of these words are a side or facet to the gem we call love, humility is a dimension of this Godlike love we are to live.

On one occasion Jesus not only demonstrated this kind of love but also shared a series of parables to make His point.

📖 Let us first set the stage by reading the preamble, in Luke 14:1–6, and answering these questions:

Whose house is Jesus at? _____

What is Jesus there to do? _____

What were the Pharisees doing? _____

Jesus knew He'd been invited for a "gotcha meal." He was well aware of his hosts' ulterior motives in having Him join them for the Sabbath meal. What they didn't know was that the table was about to be turned on them.

After healing the man with dropsy and silencing His critics, Jesus notices how the guests at this party choose for themselves places of honor at which to sit. He uses this jostling for the best seats to speak of hospitality and humility—two keystones in the kingdom of God.

📖 Read the Parable of the Humbled Servant in Luke 14:7–11.

As at a dinner party at the home of a high-powered politician, the guests invited to this meal were there to see and be seen. They were the movers and shakers of their day, and where they sat in proximity to the host said a lot about their social status. But rather than wait humbly for the host to seat them, these guests took it upon themselves to decide their positions.

It's hard to imagine the importance placed upon the seating arrangements in this story because we don't live in a society ruled so strictly by shame, honor, and purity. It is safe to say that outside the temple, there was no more significant place to demonstrate one's acceptance than table fellowship or eating together.

The Pharisees were the purity police of their day, so what were some of these purity laws?

📖 Read Leviticus 21:16–20 and answer the questions.

What was the occasion for offering food mentioned in verse 21?

_____

_____

How had the Pharisees changed the intent of this law?

_____

_____

The law concerned the purity of the one making sacrifice in the temple. However, the Pharisees twisted this law to make it apply to fellowship at the dinner table. Thus, the man Jesus healed prior to the meal would have been excluded because of his imperfection. By implication, those seeking places of honor at the meal deemed themselves to be perfect and unblemished. Summarize what Jesus says to these men of vanity (v. 11).

_____

_____

_____

If we think that because we've gone on mission trips, faithfully served on church committees, or made sacrifices above and beyond the call of duty, we will somehow receive rank in heaven, we may be surprised. Jesus says it is best to humble ourselves. In what ways do you seek to humble yourself?

_____

_____

"Happy are people who are humble, because they will inherit the earth."

Matthew 5:5 (CEV)

I truly appreciate the practice my mother insisted upon as I grew up of giving the largest piece of pie to my father "because he made it possible for us to have the pie." Now, I didn't want to give my father that big piece of pie; I wanted that piece for myself. But it was good training for placing others first. Likewise, at church dinners my sister and I were taught to wait until those in wheelchairs and using walkers or canes went first in line (which was certainly against the prevailing teaching that children go first). From this we learned what a great feeling it is to put other's needs before our own. In a surprising twist, Jesus turns His sharp tongue toward His host.

Read His words in verses 12–14.

The rule of reciprocity was alive as much then as it is today in political, business, and social circles. The host had invited only those from whom he could expect a return gesture, much like inviting children to your child's birthday party whom you expect invitations from when their birthdays come around. But Jesus once again brings His message full circle—back to the blemished and imperfect. Hospitality should be extended to those who can least afford to return the favor, who possess little social status, or who are labeled as outside the acceptable. For when does Jesus say the favor will be returned (v. 14)?

_____

_____

Upon hearing this, a Pharisee exclaims, *"Blessed is anyone who will eat bread in the kingdom of God!"* Luke records the Parable of the Great Supper in Luke 14:16–24 as Jesus' response. This parable mirrors in many ways the Parable of the Wedding Feast in Matthew 22:2–14. Compare the two, noting these differences:

Who was the wedding feast parable directed to? _____

When in Jesus' ministry was the great supper parable told?

_____

What happens to the messengers in the wedding feast parable?

_____

What happens when the invitations are rejected in the great supper parable?

_____

_____

In both Matthew's version and in Luke's, this parable presents the kingdom of God including those considered outcasts. However, when placed within the context of the Pharisaic meal in Luke, the hubris of the Pharisees is made all the more evident and the need for humility all the more pronounced. As the last words in this parable declare, those who lift themselves up may find they are left without an invitation at all.

Did You Know?

TABLE MANNERS

Table fellowship in Judaism was a complex issue for the observant Jew, especially those of the pharisaical party. Jacob Neusner has studied the rabbinical traditions of the Pharisees and he notes that of the 341 rulings that go back to the Pharisees, 229 are related to table fellowship. For this reason he says the Pharisees might be considered an "eating club!" (Jacob Neusner, From *Politics to Piety: The Emergence of Pharisaic Judaism*)

CHILD'S PLAY

I f we think the problem of pride is one only the religiously pious struggle with, this next account may change that.

📖 Read Matthew 18:1–5.

Ambition and pride are close relatives. It is easy for us to confuse healthy ambition with prideful attempts to climb ahead. Jesus recognizes sinful ambition creeping into the hearts of the disciples, and He quickly counters this by pointing to a humble child. Some call this the chapter of the child because, although Matthew never describes the scene being filled with little children, it is easy to picture children from nearby Galilee perched on Jesus' knee and playing carefree at His feet. What do you think it means to *"change and become like children"*?

_____

_____

_____

Children, by means of their status with adults, assume a position of humility. Being children of God, we likewise must assume a position of humility, not only toward God but also toward each other. No child is loved more than another, thought of more highly than another, or placed before another. To think we can garner more of God's attention or love by becoming the "greatest" is to misunderstand God's universal and impartial love. Yet when we humble ourselves and choose to lift others up, I imagine God's heart swelling with pride in us just like any parent with multiple children. Jesus continues with the child illustrations in verses 6–7.

What happens to those who cause a child to stumble?

_____

_____

Some child advocates suggest that these verses support laws against child violence. Although it is easy to see this connection, we must not forget that Jesus is speaking to the disciples about being like little children. The implication is that this admonition is not only for those who cause children to stumble and fall but also against anyone who causes God's adult children to stumble in their faith. This interpretation then allows us to read the next graphic warning within context.

📖 Read verses 8–9.

Was Jesus speaking literally about cutting off a hand or foot? If not, what could He have meant?

_____

_____

_____

Once again Jesus uses hyperbole to make an eternally significant point. If we are talking about causing someone to stumble and lose faith, this is a crime with eternal consequences. Jesus says it is better for this person to cut off a part of his body that allowed the stumbling to happen than to suffer God's wrath for eternity. Of course, we cannot cut out our hearts and minds, so it is clear this is not what Jesus is advocating. Rather, He wants us to understand the seriousness of leading even one of His children (both the young in age and the young of heart) astray. I don't know about you, but this thought causes me much humility.

📖 The introduction to this next parable says it all. Read Luke 18:9. To whom is this parable addressed?

_____

📖 Continue reading the Parable of the Pharisee and the Publican (tax collector) in verses 10–14.

The Pharisee in this parable exemplified a particularly offensive form of pride, haughtiness, evidenced by a superior manner toward inferiors. It is one thing to think we are super, but it is quite another to think we are superior.

We've become a society obsessed with self-esteem. We no longer allow children to lose in a playground game because we are afraid of bruising their self-worth. Of course, God wants us to be proud of ourselves when we've done something well, and He wants us to see ourselves as He does—valuable and loved. But there is a difference between a healthy self-image and a haughty self-esteem. The Pharisee considered himself righteous before God. He was also morally indignant when he compared himself to the tax collector. The tax collector, on the other hand, considered himself sinful and unworthy of God's mercy. He approached God with humility and a need for grace.

Fill in the blanks from this quote from verse 14 (NIV).

For everyone who _____ himself will be _____, and he who _____ himself will be _____.

Again we hear the admonition to humble ourselves or find ourselves humbled. It's a concept as simple as child's play.

GOD TALK

This difficult parable has confounded interpreters through the years, and you even may have heard it preached with those contrasting points of view. As we have learned to do before, we will take our lead from the context in which it is found.

The chapter begins with the beloved Lord's Prayer, which teaches us to go to God, our Father, with our needs. Jesus then shares this parable.

📖 Read it in Luke 11:5–8.

It is one thing to think we are super, but it is quite another to think we are superior.

Discipleship Part Three

DAY THREE

Many have interpreted this parable to be about persistence in prayer, but the Lord's Prayer that precedes it and the instructions following it to ask, seek, and knock do not support this. There is nothing in the Lord's Prayer about coming consistently before God, although we should indeed pray often.

📖 Read verses 9–10, which follow the parable. Note that they do not say we are to ask repeatedly.

The confusion comes in the translation of the word often rendered *persistence* or *importunity*, which can also mean "because of his shamelessness." God is shameless, pure, and holy. If we use this second meaning, the parable changes from one about persistence in asking for what we need to one about the honor of God being the reason for filling the man's need. With this translation we hear a consistent message. Place the letter of the three messages with the three parts of the narrative, as follows:

A. Because of God's honor, He will meet our needs.
B. God, our Father, whom we honor as hallowed, desires for us to come to Him with our needs.
C. God will be consistent and faithful in meeting our need.

_____ The Lord's Prayer
_____ The friend at midnight
_____ Ask, seek, and knock

📖 Finish reading this narrative with verses 11–13, which includes two more parabolic images.

In the first image God is compared to what? _____
In the second God is compared to what? _____
Verse 13 gives the interpretation for these parables. What is the gift the Father will give those who ask, seek, and knock? _____

God invites us to come to Him with our needs as a child with a Father, and because God is a God of honor, a God of consistent character, He will answer even our prayers uttered at midnight. When we ask, seek, and knock at the door of God's heart, He will answer because of His goodness, and that answer will come by way of the Holy Spirit.

Some have the impression that prayer is a New Testament thing. But God's people have always been people of prayer. Jesus grew up as a good Jewish boy, studying and memorizing the prayer book of His people, the book of Psalms. It does for us today the same as it did for the Jewish people through the ages—it puts words to our hearts' cries.

Here is a list of psalms by category, which you may wish to turn to when your own words seem insufficient.

Confession of sin: 32, 51, 38, 106, 130
Asking for guidance: 25, 119, 86, 123
Desire for deliverance: 17, 28, 31, 54, 59, 61, 69, 70, 71
For worship and praise: 8, 24, 33, 42, 45, 47, 48, 68, 95, 96, 113, 117
When discouraged: 13, 88, 89, 102, 123
Feeling fearful: 3, 4, 5, 23, 49, 55, 56, 116
Needing reassurance of God's faithfulness: 18, 21, 37, 52, 65, 81, 84, 89, 91, 103, 105, 106, 114, 139, 146, 147

When we ask, seek, and knock at the door of God's heart, He will answer because of His goodness, and that answer will come by way of the Holy Spirit.

Here are a few of my favorite verses from Psalms specifically on prayer. Place a star next to your favorite.

"May my prayer be set before you like incense;   may the lifting up of my hands be like the evening sacrifice" (Psalm 141:2 NIV).

"Hear my prayer, Lord;   listen to my cry for mercy" (Psalm 86:6 NIV).

"Therefore let all the faithful pray to you   while you may be found; surely the rising of the mighty waters   will not reach them" (Psalm 32:6 NIV).

"Evening, morning and noon   I cry out in distress,   and he hears my voice" (Psalm 55:17 NIV).

Spend your remaining time today praising God for His goodness, His consistency, and His character, upon which you can rest.

THE THREE GS

The Three *Gs*, grace, gratitude, and generosity, cover the three big areas—prayer, finances, and relationships—of a citizen's life in the kingdom of God.

The first *G* is addressed by a parable that many group with the two parables studied yesterday because it is a prayer parable. Although it addresses persistence in prayer, it is more a parable of grace. Let us see how.

📖 Read the Parable of the Persistent Widow and the Unjust Judge in Luke 18:1–8.

The comparison and contrast are stark. As bad as the unjust judge of the story is in one direction, our God is full of extreme goodness in the other. Fill in the table below; the first and last ones have been filled out for you.

Persistence demonstrates our faith in grace.

Our Just God . . .	The Unjust Judge . . .
listens when His people cry out	ignored the pleas of the widow
cares about justice for His chosen	
seeks swift justice	
looks for persistent faith	looked to avoid nagging

God in grace looks on the widow and all who cry out His name with the will to answer those prayers. The persistence of the widow says more about her faith than about the needs of the judge. God is looking for persistent prayers from His people *because* persistence in prayer says we believe God is a God of grace who will meet our needs. Persistence demonstrates our faith in that grace.

The next *G* is explored in the Parable of the Two Debtors. Perhaps more than any other parable, without context this parable would not have the power that it portrays.

📖 The parable is in Luke 7:41–43, but let us read the entire story beginning at verse 36.

We must not confuse this story with a similar one recorded in the other three Gospels. This one takes place in the home of Simon the Pharisee, in the town of Nain, as opposed to Bethany. All we know of the unnamed woman is that Simon called her a sinner, probably a prostitute, and she was not invited by him but came because of her great need.

It must have taken incredible courage to enter the home of the Pharisee, knowing the punishment for her sins was stoning. Her need for mercy propelled her to fall at Jesus' feet, a sign of humility, and in this lowly place the weight of her unworthiness poured forth in her tears.

Simon, on the other hand, exhibited no courage whatsoever. Indeed, he'd invited Jesus to dine with him, but not because of respect or any desire to hear what Jesus had to say. He had such little esteem for Jesus, he neglected to offer Him the customary water for washing His sandaled feet. He offered no anointing oil nor the expected kiss of welcome.

By contrast, the lowly and sinful woman was too ashamed to kiss Jesus' cheek and instead kissed His feet, washed them with her tears, and anointed them with oil, which probably cost all that she had.

Have you ever participated in a foot-washing ceremony? If you have, describe how it made you feel.

_____

_____

_____

I've participated in a foot washing, and it was the most humbling thing I've ever experienced. Although no words are exchanged, volumes are said. The woman in our story never utters a word, and yet the communication between Jesus and her must have filled the room. I can picture her not wanting to look at Jesus, yet being drawn to steal a glance. What she would have seen in His eyes must have melted her heart.

Such a display Simon could not stand for. Jesus knew Simon's closed heart and offered this parable to pry it open.

We have not approached many parables as allegories—in which the elements of the story represent or stand for something else—because in some cases that seems to stretch the parable beyond its intent. But here Jesus makes it clear that is His intent.

"If this man were a prophet, he would know who is touching him and what kind of woman she is—that she is a sinner."

Luke 7:39b (NIV)

📖 Read the parable in verses 40–43 and match the characters from the story to the descriptions.

Jesus   Debtor owing 50 denairi
Simon   Debtor owing 500 denaris
Sinful woman   The creditor

With skill Jesus forced Simon to indict himself. Without a doubt, Simon recognized himself as the man in the story who was least grateful. We do not know if Simon repented, but we do know the woman's sins were forgiven and that she left a free and grateful woman. What causes you to be most grateful? What has God forgiven you for that has made you so grateful you'd fall to your knees before Him and pour out your gratitude in tears of joy?

_____

_____

_____

The final *G* is generosity and is depicted in the famous parable about the camel and the eye of a needle. A rich young man comes to Jesus with a question. Recognizing Jesus as a good teacher, he asks Him what he must do to inherit eternal life. It is an academic question, but Jesus won't let him stay in that academic world. He wants to get to the heart of the issue, so Jesus first throws the academic off his game by asking a language question.

📖 Read this interchange in Luke 18:18–25.

When on a Christian journalists' tour of Israel in 2009, I saw an actual needle's eye (you can see a picture of it on my website (www.CheriCowell.com) in my Holy Land photo gallery). It is a small gate or door, elevated about three feet from the floor. The door is so small that a camel would have to be unladened to enter it. The point is simple. A rich man, by comparison, would need to unladen himself of the riches he tightly holds in his heart and hand so he might enter the door to the kingdom. What must you and I unladen ourselves from so we might freely enter through the small door into the kingdom of God?

_____

_____

_____

Discipleship Part Three

DAY FIVE

ROCKS AND STONES

As we bring our study of the parables in the Gospels to a close and move toward those in the remaining New Testament, we must look at one more parabolic image. It is an image with three applications that has inspired Christians through the centuries to hold tight to their faith, and at the same time it has divided Christians.

📖 Read Matthew 16:15–18. What is this image?

_____

The church is divided over whom Jesus was referencing when He told Peter, *"On this rock I will build my church."* Some say Peter is that rock, and this position is used to support apostolic succession for ordination of priests and bishops—meaning that only those who can trace their lineage to Peter (and the other disciples) have inherited spiritual, ecclesiastical, and sacramental authority. The other position is that Jesus was referencing the faith that Peter just confessed as the rock upon which He would build His church.

📖 Read Psalm 18:2. Who is the rock in this psalm?_____

📖 Next, look up Isaiah 28:16.
Who is the stone laid in Zion?_____

Fill in the blanks for this quote from this passage:
A precious _____ for a sure _____

Jesus used this comparison of the rock and the cornerstone when speaking of the stumbling block His own reign would be for some people.

📖 Read Matthew 21:42–44.

Jesus is quoting Psalm 118:22, but Isaiah 8:13–15 must not have been far from His mind. Read it now.

This Scripture tells us that the Lord Almighty himself will be a holy place. As recorded in the book of John, following the miracle at Cana where Jesus turns water into wine, Jesus goes to the temple for Passover. There He finds people selling cattle, sheep, and doves in the temple courtyard for sacrifice. Jesus is incensed that His father's house was nothing more to these men than a place of commerce. Jesus overturns the tables and the cages of these merchants, and when questioned as to what authority He was appealing, Jesus responds with this parable.

📖 Read John 2:19–22.

The Jews understood Jesus to mean the temple from which Jesus had just driven the merchants. This temple had been under construction since its last razing forty-six years earlier, and it still wasn't finished. Now they heard Jesus say He could rebuild it in three days! But Jesus wasn't speaking of the stone building before Him. He was speaking of a Temple built from the Rock Foundation, who formed the world, the Chief Cornerstone in the kingdom, the Temple that would be destroyed—or so Satan would think. This Temple housed the Precious Stone upon which the Church would be built, and after three days that Temple would rise from the ashes. Today that Temple stands. Paul, in his letter to the church at Ephesus, takes all of these images and wraps them into one tightly woven passage.

📖 Read Ephesians 2:19–22, printed below, and underline every reference to a foundation, cornerstone, building, temple, and dwelling.

Consequently, you are no longer foreigners and strangers, but fellow citizens with God's people and also members of his household, built on the foundation of the apostles and prophets, with Christ Jesus himself as the chief cornerstone. In him the whole building is joined together and rises to become a holy temple in the Lord. And in him you too are being built together to become a dwelling in which God lives by his Spirit (NIV).

What do you think it means that we are *"being built together to become a dwelling"* place for God?

_____

_____

_____

_____

_____

Often we think of our faith and the Christian life as a solitary event. It is about the decision "I make" and the way "I choose" to live out "my faith." But Christianity is not a solitary act. *"In him the whole building is joined together"*; that is, all of us together form the *"holy temple."* In the remaining weeks of this study, we will look at how twelve men became a temple and how those twelve grew into a kingdom by re-examining the parables Jesus taught and building upon them as they sought to become worthy of the one who now dwelt within them. May you and I be so bold.

Notes

Parables of the Church

FROM ACTS AND PAUL'S EPISTLES

ACTING IN FAITH

We now move from the Gospels to the book of Acts and the rest of the New Testament, and it is striking to note that the parable, as Jesus used it, disappears. The disciples spent three years under the tutelage of the greatest parable preacher who ever lived, and yet they did not create one new parable in their own ministries that followed. Instead, what we often find are extensions of previously preached parables or parable sequels. These parable sequels rely heavily on the listener's memory of the parable as told by the Lord. Then it uses that memory as a springboard to expound upon the point Jesus made concerning living the kingdom way. Paul was the expert at this, and we will look at several sequels he created. We will also look at something new the disciples bring to the study of parables—parabolic miracles and actions. In these, the event not only has import because of the miracle itself but because of the parabolic symbolism that goes beyond the mere miracle. For example, from the beginning of the book of Acts, we have the miracle of Pentecost, which stands on its own as an amazing miracle. But this miracle also has layers of symbolism that move beyond the miracle and point to new realities for kingdom living. The New Testament is filled with many parabolic miracles or events that we will examine together.

One of the ways the disciples actually followed in Jesus' footsteps was in the area of parabolic figures of speech, such as similes, metaphors, allegories, and illustrations or imagery. This is where the disciples most closely model their Teacher's parabolic ways. Most of what we will study in the coming weeks will fall into this category.

Let us begin with the book of Acts, also known as the Acts of the Apostles because it outlines the actions of the followers of Christ after Jesus' death and resurrection. Our first parabolic image is that of baptism.

📖 Read Acts 1:1–5, especially noting verse 5.

📖 Luke, the author of the book of Acts, makes reference here to a passage in his first book. Read Luke 3:16.

John's baptism symbolized repentance and the washing away of a sinful life. A few verses later in Luke (v. 21), Jesus is baptized to symbolize His full identity with a sinful humanity, although He never sinned. Now Luke takes that symbolism a step further in Acts with the baptism of the Holy Spirit, which is an immersion in the one who is living water.

📖 Look up John 7:38.

When you and I are baptized, we are identifying with an "already" and a "not-yet" event. This outward symbol illustrates that we are receiving on the inside the water of life. This is the inauguration of the kingdom of God in us.

📖 Read the prophecy in Zechariah 14:7–9.

The inauguration of this promise has taken place, but the fulfillment is yet to come when the Lord will rule over all the earth. Until that day, we hold fast to the reality that the promised kingdom is here.

📖 Where does Luke 17:21 tell us it is?

_____

_____

It flows within us and out from us at the point of our baptism.
As we've already said, the miracle of Pentecost is also a parabolic event.

📖 Read Acts 2:1–4 and list the three symbolic images given in just these few verses.

_____

_____

📖 The wind ties us back to Genesis 2:7. Who is the wind?

_____

📖 The breath of life blew across the crowd on the day of Pentecost, and tongues of fire sat upon them. This second reference is from Exodus 19:16–18. How did the Lord God appear to Moses?

_____

_____

In combining these two symbols, Luke is saying the Spirit of God, as symbolized by fire, was the cause of the miracle in which the visitors from several nationalities heard the Good News spoken in their own languages.

When you and I are baptized, we are identifying with an "already" and a "not-yet" event. This outward symbol illustrates that we are receiving on the inside the water of life. This is the inauguration of the kingdom of God in us.

In just two short chapters in Acts, we've seen a parabolic miracle, parabolic images, and a parabolic event. These parables have shaped the way the Christian church has seen itself and its mission through the ages. How have these images, symbols, and references shaped or changed the view of your own baptism and your participation in the spreading of the Good News of the kingdom?

_____

_____

_____

_____

MORE ACTS OF FAITH

Acts 3 begins with a miracle parable. Read it in verses 1–10.

The Beautiful Gate was the most popular entrance to the temple, and therefore a good place for the beggar to sit and make his pleas. It was also a good place for a miracle with a clear message. The key to unlocking this parable is in the reference to gold from Psalm 19:10. What is better than gold and honey according to this verse?

_____

_____

Peter and John understood Jesus as the embodiment of the law and decrees of God. They understood that as His representatives they had something more powerful to offer the man than simple gold or silver. They knew that the power to heal, to break bonds, and even to defeat death was contained in the name of Jesus. When you utter the name of Jesus, do you believe this too? When you encounter those in need, are you offering only gold, or are you also offering them the gift that is most valuable—Jesus?

When hauled before the Sanhedrin, Peter takes one of Jesus' metaphors and spells out the connection so it cannot be missed.

📖 Read Acts 4:8–12.

You may recall that Jesus prophesied this of himself in Matthew 21:42–44.

Later Peter would make a clear connection between these two in 1 Peter 2:7. What kind of stone is described in this passage? _____

📖 Jesus is described as a capstone; the large stone uniting two pillars to form an arch. This capstone must be perfectly balanced in order to hold the two sides together. What are the two sides? Read Ephesians 2:19–22 for the answer.

_____

_____

Foreigners and strangers are the Gentiles, and God's people are the Jews. Jesus is the capstone that unites these two pillars forming a *"holy temple"* unto God. When Stephen was brought before the Sadducees, he further illuminated the use of the tabernacle and temple as signs and symbols of the Lord Jesus.

📖 Read Stephen's bold confession in Acts 7:46–50.

📖 Look up 1 Corinthians 3:16. Where is the temple of God, and where does He dwell today?

_____

_____

Jesus is the cornerstone the builders rejected, the capstone uniting Jews and Gentiles into a holy temple—a temple not formed by human hands but hearts united in love.

Jesus is the cornerstone the builders rejected, the capstone uniting Jews and Gentiles into a holy temple—a temple not formed by human hands but hearts united in love.

One of the greatest parabolic images of the New Testament is the sheet in Peter's dream. As with our Gospel parables, this dream imagery cannot be extracted from its context. So to fully understand this important symbol of the kingdom, read about the previous events in Acts 10:1–8.

📖 Now read Peter's dream in Acts 10:9–16 and answer the questions.

How was the sheet coming out of heaven?

_____

What types of animals were on the sheet?

_____

What was Peter's protest concerning?

_____

What was God's response?

_____

_____

The rest of this story, as outlined in verses 17–48, not only gives the full interpretation of the dream but also the application. The four corners of the sheet represent the four corners of the world, and the Jews considered the animals with cloven hoofs and reptiles to be unclean. When Peter protested God's direct order to eat these animals, he was saying he would not do what he knew to be wrong in God's eyes. Sometimes, however, what we think is wrong may actually be right.

Peter was a good Jew, and he'd been taught that salvation was for the Jews and the Jews only. But there was no denying the God-orchestrated circumstances surrounding his invitation to Cornelius' home. Peter readily made the connection to his dream and the houseful of Gentiles before him, ready to receive the Good News.

📖 Read Acts 10:28.

Because of Peter's willingness to set aside his views and listen anew to God, the Holy Spirit swept through the home of Cornelius, and, by extension, made you and me part of God's family today.

What belief(s) are you holding tight to today that God is making clear you must change? Are there people you believe to be unacceptable that God is saying are acceptable in His sight? I've certainly struggled with this. At times the church has taught that entire groups of people are unacceptable, but God made it known in this image that anyone can be made clean by the blood of the Lamb. All deserve to hear and a chance to receive the Good News. Make note of those people or groups of people God is bringing to you mind:

_____

_____

_____

_____

Pray that God will give you a vision of what His kingdom will look like when those people are a part of it, and ask Him to give you a heart like Peter's—a heart willing to go to whomever He sends you.

BEWARE, LITTLE SHEEP

As a child I loved the story of Peter's escape from prison. It has drama, mystery, and suspense—all the elements of a good story. What I didn't know as a child were the layers of symbolism this one miracle brought to the Christian faith. Read this great miracle parable in Acts 12:1–11.

The allegory is so obvious to us today because we've filled songs, hymns, and paintings with the symbols. Our sins have imprisoned us, while faith in Christ sets us free. Faith breaks the chains holding us hostage and opens the doors to dark cells, bringing us into the presence of Christ. As the song goes, "My chains are gone, I've been set free. My God, my Savior has ransomed me."[3]

But not all will hear this Good News. What does Acts 13:51 tell us Paul and Barnabas did when they encountered those who refused to believe?

_____

_____

Faith breaks the chains holding us hostage and opens the doors to dark cells, bringing us into the presence of Christ.

A similar parabolic action was repeated in Acts 18:6. This was similar to the instructions given the disciples by Jesus in Matthew 10:14. By shaking dust from their feet (or clothes in Paul's case), the disciples shook off responsibility for the receipt of the message, which now lay on the floor at the foot of the nonbeliever. You and I are never responsible for the results of our efforts to share the gospel; we are only responsible for sharing it.

Paul is saying to the Jews that if they reject this open door or gate, which is Jesus, he will extend that invitation by faith to the Gentiles. This door of faith has now swung wide open for all those who will hear and believe.

The next three images are examples of the parable extension or sequel. Paul, knowing of Jesus' description of himself as a door in John 10, extends that simile in Acts 14:27. This time the door is called what?

_____

Paul is saying to the Jews that if they reject this open door or gate, which is Jesus, he will extend that invitation by faith to the Gentiles. This door of faith has now swung wide open for all those who will hear and believe.

📖 Read these further references Paul made to the door:

2 Corinthians 2:12
Colossians 4:3

In Paul's next parable sequel, he creatively weaves Jesus' teaching about the heavy burdens the Pharisees placed on their people (Matthew 23:4) with His teaching of the easy yoke (Matthew 11:30).

📖 Read Galatians 5:1 and explain how Paul expounded upon Jesus' teachings.

_____

_____

_____

The question in Galatians was whether the Gentile Christians also had to be circumcised. Paul is adamant that freedom in Christ is real freedom. It is freedom from burdensome laws and a sin-marked life. However, it does not mean Christians are free to do whatever we please. There is still a yoke we must carry, a yoke that unites us to Christ and His kingdom ways. But that yoke is light compared to the burden we must otherwise carry as slaves to this world of sin.

📖 In Acts 20:28–31, what two parables is Paul recalling from Matthew and John?

_____

_____

_____

The good shepherd (John 10:11) cares for His sheep and has placed caretakers in positions of leadership over His flock. He's done this because there are wolves hiding in sheep's clothing among the sheep (Matthew 7:15). No doubt when Paul wrote this he had in mind Jeremiah 23:1–2 and his own merciless pursuit of Christians prior to his conversion.

I am sad to say some of the deepest and most damaging wounds happen within the four walls of the church. I have been severely wounded by people professing the Christian faith, and I know many who've left their faith because of their own hurts experienced there. If the church or those within the church have wounded you, let me first say how sorry I am. This never was the way it was supposed to be. God intended for the church to be a safe haven, but as this passage tells us, God is also realistic. Paul, once having been duped by Satan, knows how crafty Satan is, and Paul warned the church to be on guard. What better way to defeat God's plans than to stage a coup from within? As sheep in God's flock, we must guard our hearts and minds, bringing all things and all people before Him. Remember the Parable of the Good Shepherd—He knows His sheep by touch and He calls them by name. The Good Shepherd can tell us who is who, if we will ask. But asking sometimes reveals what we know in our hearts to be true, that this world still belongs to Satan, and God's kingdom, although inaugurated, is not yet fully realized. This means that good people will still suffer, and often at the hands of those who are supposed to be our protectors, our shepherds. Thus is the case with our next illustration. Paul is standing trial before the high priest when he proclaims his innocence and the priest orders him punched. Paul then uses a loaded phrase, which the high priest no doubt recognizes as originating with Jesus.

📖 Read this exchange in Acts 23:1–5.

Of course this references Matthew 23, in which Jesus called the religious leaders whitewashed sepulchers hiding dead men's bones. Ananias's actions betrayed his position; therefore, Paul didn't recognize him as being the high priest. Do our actions betray who we say we are? Do we need a bumper sticker on our cars to tell people we are Christians, or can they tell that by how we act?

PAUL'S EPISTLES

Today we continue our look at the parable extensions of Paul, but now we move to his many letters. The first one we will look at some might consider his signature; it is what he is best known for.

📖 Read Romans 11:17–24. Which parable of Jesus is Paul referencing?

_____

_____

_____

Paul uses here the teaching of the Parable of the Vine from John 15:1–16 about being grafted into and nourished by the root of the vine for kingdom living. This promise was previously understood to be for the Jews, but Paul uses it to tell how the Gentiles have been grafted into that same promise of Abraham. This is perhaps the best example of a parable sequel because it clearly builds upon the Parable of Jesus yet offers a part two to the story. Without Paul's explanation, many of us today would not be able to explain what took place between Jesus' ministry and the expansion of the gospel into the entire world.

So significant was this imagery for the new Gentile Christians that they took the symbol of an olive branch as their icon. Recently, pottery with the grafted-in symbol was discovered on Mount Zion in Israel, dating from the second century. Today this symbol is posted on the storefronts of Christian merchants in Israel and on the doorposts of the homes of Christians there who want to show their rootedness in the Jewish faith.

The menorah at the top of the image represents God's covenant with the people of Israel. The Star of David in the middle, comprised of interlocking triangles of the letter D (delta or) from the Greek alphabet, symbolized the name of Israel's greatest king and is a reminder that the son of David, Yeshua, will sit on the throne of David. The fish at the bottom has a rich history of identification with the believer. It was a common symbol for believers because the Greek word for fish (*ichthys*) was used as an acronym for "Yeshua, Son of God, Savior."

Next we turn to Paul's letter to the Corinthian church. In 1 Corinthians 3:9–15 we find reference to two more of Jesus' parables. Can you guess which ones?

_____

_____

_____

Two parables come to mind when reading Paul's teaching on foundations and on using proper materials—the Parable of the Wise and Foolish Builders in Matthew 7:21–28 and the Parable of the Two Builders from Luke 14:25–30. However, Paul takes the images further. Here someone is building upon another man's foundation.

In 1 Corinthians 3:9, who does Paul say is God's building? _____
In verse 11, who is the foundation? _____

Paul cautions us when building upon that foundation to use materials that will stand the test of time. Which parable of Jesus is Paul referencing?

_____

_____

This is a reference to the Parable of the Two Builders about counting the cost so as to finish the building project. What do you think these costly materials might be?

_____

_____

Again we must look to our context for answers. The church at Corinth was quarreling over who was the greater teacher and leader, Paul or Apollos, another popular preacher. I don't know about you, but I've witnessed many church quarrels. Some were over little things like changing the carpet, and some over big things like changing the style of worship. To some people, changing the carpet was just as big a deal as changing worship style.

Paul says in 1 Corinthians 3:1–9 that the quarrel over Paul and Apollos is silly because neither he nor Apollos is greater. Each had a job to do, but it was God—not either one of them—who produced the results. Paul then delivers the parable sequel in the verses that follow.

📖 Read 1 Corinthians 3:18–23 and answer the question.

If foolish building materials are wisdom from this world, what might the wise materials be?

_____

_____

This proverb was probably in the back of Paul's mind. Write Proverbs 16:16 here:

_____

_____

_____

Earlier in the letter, Paul makes a startling connection. In 1 Corinthians 1:22–25 who does Paul say wisdom is? _____

Jesus is wisdom personified. He is everything we ought to be. Taking all of this together, Paul is saying that what may seem like foolishness in the world—forgiveness, humility, sacrifice, weakness—are the precious stones, the gems of wisdom, that form strong temples.

Sadly, much quarreling within the body of Christ is over foolish things, things that will not stand the test of time. Frankly, neither the color carpet nor the style of worship we choose today will matter in eternity. If we'd take a step back and lean less on our own understanding, we'd begin to see the foolishness of our ways. It is having God's wisdom and knowledge that makes us wise and allows us to have a kingdom view of things. So go ahead, be a fool for Christ! Let His ways become your ways and you will be wise beyond years. Perhaps in this way we might learn to be less quarrelsome as the body of Christ.

RAGS TO RICHES

Because of Paul's writings there are a few parables of Christ's that have grown in meaning. On their own in the Gospels they spoke to us, but now those same words speak more loudly through the megaphone of Paul's teaching. Such is the case with references to clothes.

📖 Read Romans 13:11–14. What clothes are we to "put off" and what are we to *put on*?

_____

_____

Two parables of Jesus' come to mind when I hear this reference to clothes. The first is the Parable of the Wedding Banquet, in which the man refused to wear the wedding clothes sent to him by the bridegroom. The second is the New Patch on the Old Garment. When I hear both of these parables as taught by our Lord, I am reminded of this teaching in Romans—that I must choose to put on the righteousness of Christ and put off those things that are

So go ahead, be a fool for Christ! Let His ways become your ways and you will be wise beyond years.

Parables of the Church

DAY FIVE

not of God. I can't simply put a new patch on those old clothes and wear those. No, those old clothes won't do. List from verse 13 what those old clothes are:

_____

_____

I was shocked to see dissension or quarreling and jealousy listed with those other ugly hand-me-downs. Certainly those sins aren't as dirty as that other laundry, or are they? Paul says they are. In fact, when we refuse to see dissension and jealousy as equally filthy to the rags of sexual immorality and orgies, we may convince ourselves that these old clothes are okay. After all, they *are* comfortable. But we are told we must give them up if we are to attend the wedding banquet.

📖 Read Isaiah 61:10 and answer the questions.

What is the garment we must put on?

_____

What is the robe we must wear?

_____

What do you think this means?

_____

We have been salvaged from the trash heap of sin.

We have been salvaged from the trash heap of sin. To use the clothing analogy, our rags have been replaced with clothing of rich fabric because of Christ's sacrifice. No longer do our rags identify us; instead, we are clothed in robes of "right-ness" if only we will choose to put them on. Choosing to put them on means we must first take off the old clothes and stand bare before God. That is the scary part for most of us. It is uncomfortable having someone see the real us. We are afraid of condemnation and criticism, but that is not what God has in store for us. When we finally say we are tired of our old rags, God opens His closet and pulls out the most beautiful robes we have ever laid eyes upon. He hands them to us each and every day. Have you chosen to put on your new robe, or are you still clinging to your old clothes? As we turn to our next parable sequel, we see that Paul has some harsh words and what some might harsh treatment for those in the church who refuse to take off their old garments.

📖 Read 1 Corinthians 5:6–8.

In verses 1–5 we learn there is member of the church who is sleeping with his father's wife, yet this congregation is boasting of their moral uprightness! To put it lightly, Paul is incensed. Although this man and this congregation know that what he is doing is repugnant to God, they are choosing to look the other way. Is anyone cringing with me right now? Taking Jesus' Parable of the Leavened Bread in Matthew 16:6–12; 13:33–35, Paul addresses the situation in the Corinthian church. Summarize Paul's point.

_____

_____

_____

_____

_____

To allow even one person to refuse to acknowledge his sin and change his ways is to contaminate the whole batch. The reality is, we are not individuals who get to choose what we want to do and how we want to live without consequences to the body. The whole body of Christ is leavened with just a small measure of leavening.

In 1 Corinthians 5:9–13, Paul tells us just what should happen if this member of the household of faith refuses to repent. It is tough to hear. But Paul makes it clear this is meant for only some people. Who does Paul say this judgment is reserved for? _____

We must be careful to apply such harsh treatment only to those who know the truth. The Holy Spirit reveals truth, and its possession is a sign of spiritual maturity. Therefore, it is obvious the man in this community of faith was at a level of spiritual maturity that he could be held accountable. When we refuse to hold the spiritually mature among us accountable, we are potentially doing more harm to the cause of Christ than the person who brings the leaven to the batch.

Notes

Prepared with Paul

PARABLES AND PARABLE SEQUELS

SOWING SEEDS

One of Paul's favorite parables from Jesus was that of the sower and the seed, which we studied from Matthew 13. Read Paul's sequel in 2 Corinthians 9:6–11. Jesus' message was about the kingdom. What was the point of Paul's use of this parable imagery?

_____

_____

_____

As we read in verses 1–5 of this chapter, Paul is addressing the subject of giving in kingdom living. As was the case, this community of believers was about to give a large offering to support a start-up church in neighboring Macedonia. It is interesting to note that none of the churches Paul started would be considered wealthy by today's standards. The Corinthians were giving out of their poverty, so one might expect Paul to speak to this hardship. Instead, he challenges them to give with joy, out of glad and generous hearts. Verse 10 is a direct link to Jesus' parable. The sower in Jesus' parable is not identified, but who does Paul say the sower is?

_____

_____

Who supplies the seed?

_____

If Jesus is the sower and He provides the seed, what is our role?

_____

_____

When we scatter the seed, which in this case is to give generously out of a generous heart, what does verse 11 say God will do for us?

_____

_____

In a similar way, Paul speaks to the idea that those in ministry should do so out of the goodness of their hearts, not expecting to be paid.

📖 Read 1 Corinthians 9:9–11. According to Paul, why should those who plow and thresh receive monetary support?

_____

_____

📖 For the sake of the harvest, the sower and reaper should be supported financially. Read 2 Timothy 2:6–7, which gives more support for this concept. Who is the *"hardworking farmer"* (NIV)?_____

Paul tells Timothy, a young minister of the gospel, that those who suffer for Christ's sake should also receive a share of the crops. Both of my grandfathers were Methodist circuit pastors. Back in those days, pastors weren't paid much, and so the churches they served would gather together quarterly for a "pounding." As my grandmother described it, "Everyone would bring from the bounty of their crops a 'pound of this or that.'" She said she learned how to stretch those canned goods and slaughtered animals until the next pounding, when their pantry would be filled once again. I'd say these faithful people were living out Paul's teaching. Although our pastors today are often paid well, how can we live out this teaching?

_____

_____

_____

Next let's look at how Paul applies the sowing and reaping imagery to another important aspect of kingdom life—that of the spiritual life versus a life of the flesh.

📖 Read Galatians 6:7–9.and summarize Paul's point.

_____

_____

It would be silly to think we could plant corn and harvest turnips, but when we sow fleshly deeds such as greed, gossip, and ingratitude, why are we surprised when that is what we reap? The last verse in this section addresses those of us who have been sowing the right things but our harvest is still weak. How does verse 9 encourage us?

_____

_____

It would be silly to think we could plant corn and harvest turnips, but when we sow fleshly deeds such as greed, gossip, and ingratitude, why are we surprised when that is what we reap?

With a slight twist Paul takes the seed metaphor and uses it to address one of the biggest questions believers still face today.

📖 Read this great parable sequel in 1 Corinthians 15:35–44.

According to Paul, what are our bodies? _____

When are they sown? _____

What will they become at harvest? _____

Seed bodies are what Paul calls our earthly vessels. When we die, they are sown back into the earth—dust to dust and ashes to ashes. At the resurrection our perishable bodies will become new, imperishable ones just like the one Jesus had when He was raised from the dead. On that day our old natural bodies will be gone, and we will live forever in our new spiritual bodies. Spiritual, in this sense, does not mean an earthly body. However, just like Jesus had a real body when He appeared to the disciples, so will we. The disciples saw His nail-scarred hands, and Thomas put his finger in His pierced side. Jesus even ate with them. Yet He passed through doors and clearly lived both here and at the same time in another realm. Although we do not know exactly how this will work, this parable extension from Paul offers us hope.

What is your belief about heaven and the new body you will receive? How does this parable from Paul give you hope?

_____

_____

_____

_____

BODY OF BELIEF

A most beloved parable extension of Paul's is what we call the fruit of the spirit. If you will remember, Jesus speaks about knowing a tree by its fruit in Matthew 7:16–20. In Galatians 5:22–23 Paul describes the kind of good fruit that followers of Christ will produce in their lives. There are nine different fruits. List them in the first column.

Fruit of the Spirit	Fruit of the Flesh
1.	1.
2.	2.
3.	3.
4.	4.
5.	5.
6.	6.
7.	7.
8.	8.
9.	9.
	10.

📖 Now look at Galatians 5:19 and add to the right column the fruit of the flesh (as it is listed in your Bible; some lines will have two listed together).

Looking at this list, circle the fruit your tree (life) heartily produces and underline those you do not harvest. From the remaining list, ask God to give you more of the fruit you seek and help to rid your orchard of those you do not want.

Two more of our favorites from Paul are not parable extensions at all. They are Paul's own creation. Both are descriptions of who we are in Christ and how we are to represent Him in the world.

📖 The first parable is that of living letters, found in 2 Corinthians 3:2–3. Read it now.

The context tells us that false teachers had presented the Corinthians with forged letters of recommendation in order to validate their teaching. Paul sarcastically asks if the Corithians needed papers from him or if they were satisfied in seeing the results of his teaching—the human letters of recommendation written by the Holy Spirit on the hearts of believers.

You and I don't need a sign to hang around our necks to tell others we belong to Christ. Instead, when we become followers of Christ, we become letters of recommendation to the world for the cause of Christ. Are you a positive letter of recommendation? Would others turn to Christ after reading your letter?

Paul's other parable is so much a part of our lexicon it is easy to miss its parabolic significance. However, just like with the parables his Master taught, the simplicity of this parable is also its beauty.

📖 Read the Parable of the Body of Christ in 1 Corinthians 12:12–26.

What part of the body are you?_____

Two common mistakes among Christians are (1) believing we are not as important as some other part of the body, and (2) thinking more highly of ourselves than the rest of the body. This parable makes it clear that the church, or the body of Christ, is made up of different parts that function as a whole, with every part needed and no part more important than another. From the beginning of this chapter, we learn the Corinthians were arguing about spiritual gifts and whose gift was greater. Have you ever been in a church where arguments occurred over which ministry was more important? Paul tells the Corinthian church and us that all gifts and ministries come from God and are therefore equal in value. He also instructs that when one part of the body suffers, we must weep, and when one part rejoices, we must join in on the celebration.

The question posed to you and me is, When a fellow Christian is honored, how do we react? If I were honest, I'd have to say I'm not always rejoicing. Sometimes I'm too busy focusing on "why not me?" to see the "why him or her." Is there someone in the church whose gifts or talents turn you green?

Write that person's name here. _____

How about when others are suffering—does your heart break along with their's? This tends to be a little easier for me, except when I believe they have somehow contributed to their own difficulty. I know—that's not very Christlike. But I'm just being honest. Is there someone you know who is suffering but for whom you can't quite muster full sympathy? Write that person's name here. _____

To be a member of the body of Christ means that when one limb or organ suffers or rejoices, the rest of the members must weep or leap together. This includes all people, even those about whom we experience tinges of envy and those for whom we feel unsympathetic. Therefore, ask God to help you see the two members of the body whose names you wrote above not only as equal but also essential to the life of the body.

📖 In another place Paul speaks of the body, but this time he uses another metaphor. Read 2 Corinthians 4:7 and record what the image is.

_____

_____

In this instance Paul compares our earthly bodies to earthen pottery, jars of clay. Because verse 7 begins with the word *but*, we must read what has been said before to understand what this metaphor references. Begin reading where this thought begins in verse 4. What treasure does Paul refer to?

_____

_____

_____

The light of Christ has been placed in jars of clay, our bodies. Why? Paul knew that would be the question, so he answers it in verses 8–12. In your own words, write what you think Paul is saying.

_____

_____

_____

When the pressure is on, do you crush under the weight or stand strong? When life is confusing, do you give into despair or seek contentment? When persecution is the order of the day, do you feel abandoned or hide in the arms of Jesus? And when life is draining from your veins and from the veins of those you love, do you decry death or welcome that end as a new beginning? How we handle the real life we now live in this body shines God's light or snuffs it out. Does your jar of clay have windows or a lid?

FOLLOWING AND FINISHING

One parabolic image not used by Jesus but used by Paul is the military metaphor. Jesus' Jewish audience would not have resonated with military comparisons because they could not and would not

To be a member of the body of Christ means that when one limb or organ suffers or rejoices, the rest of the members must weep or leap together.

Does your jar of clay have windows or a lid?

Prepared with Paul

DAY THREE

serve in the Roman army. But imagine the Gentiles—for whom military service would have been an honorable calling—hearing this message.

📖 Read Ephesians 6:13–17 and fill in the chart.
The Full Armor of God

The belt of	
	Righteousness
Feet fitted with readiness of the	
	Faith
Helmet of	
Sword of the Spirit is the	

Paul envisioned a warrior for Christ, ready to battle with the principalities of this world because he or she had properly suited up. Three times the word *stand* or withstand is used at the beginning of this parable. We must be ready to stand before Satan, knowing we are armored for the battle.

📖 Paul applies the military metaphor a second time. Read 2 Timothy 2:3–4. Who is your commanding officer? _____

Soldiers give up the right to do things their own ways. Instead, they pledge to do whatever their commanding officers direct them to do. They are no longer people unto themselves; their actions must now reflect those of their commanding officers. If you have enlisted in God's army, have you renounced your right to do as you please? Are you following God's commands? What would you need to change in your life if you were to follow God's orders? Mark the things in the list below that you'd need to change.

❏ My speech
❏ How I spend my free time
❏ How I spend my money
❏ How I think and talk about others
❏ How I treat "difficult people"
❏ What I see and do
❏ Who I hang out with
❏ What books, magazines, video, television, and Internet sites I view
❏ How I treat my body
❏ How I view myself

The ticker-tape parade we are leading rains down love as its confetti, and we are unfurling the banner of grace and peace.

One reality of war is the presence of captives or prisoners of war. Paul uses this analogy to paint a picture of who we are in Christ. Read 2 Corinthians 2:14. This metaphor includes a startling twist—as captives of Christ we are not in some prison or barracks, but rather we are captives in a celebratory procession. It is the image of a triumphal entry of the victorious commander and his warriors, spreading the fragrance of love, mercy, and compassion to a world needing salvation. I picture V-Day with Christ as our commanding general. The ticker-tape parade we are leading rains down love as its confetti, and we are unfurling the banner of grace and peace.

In 2 Corinthians 10:5 we see the military image used in the battle of the mind. What are we taking captive? _____

Paul says as good soldiers we demolish arguments and pretensions (NIV) and take every thought captive so as to make those thoughts obedient to Christ, our commander.

In writing to the young pastor Timothy, Paul combines the military metaphor with another of his favorites—running a good race.

📖 Read 2 Timothy 4:7.

📖 Then in 1 Corinthians 9:24–27 we get the full parable on running the race. Read this great parable now.

Anyone who has trained for a race understands the concept of making one's body a slave. When every fiber of your body screams to stop, as a runner you must must put mind over body and push through the pain. The reward is an adrenalin state that allows the runner to finish strong and possibly receive the prize. As Paul relates it , you and I are in kingdom training, and at times we must force our bodies, mind, and wills to conform to the ways of Christ. When we do, we will enter a state of contentment, even joy.

📖 Hebrews 12:1–3 is perhaps one of my favorite passages. The writer beautifully draws our attention to the finish line and our need to persevere. Read this parable and answer the questions.

What do you think the words *"pioneer and perfecter"* mean?

_____

_____

Who is the pioneer and perfecter of your faith? _____

The pioneer is the one who blazes the trail and clears the way for others, and the perfecter is the one who completes or makes perfect. In other words, Jesus began the race and He will finish it with you. If you will simply run the race, stay the course, push through the pain, and endure till you reach the end, Jesus will be at the finish line with a crown of glory in His hands for you. That is a prize worth running for.

A PERFECT IMITATION

Paul was in a Roman prison at the time he wrote his letter to the church he started at Philippi. This background gives color and texture to the images he used in the book of Philippians. The first is what Paul must have felt like chained in a dark and damp cell.

📖 Read Philippians 2:5–11. What is Jesus said to be like in verse 7?

_____

_____

> **You and I are in kingdom training, and at times we must force our bodies, mind, and wills to conform to the ways of Christ. When we do, we will enter a state of contentment, even joy.**

Prepared with Paul

DAY FOUR

Unfortunately, some translations have rendered the word *slave* as "servant." The slave analogy better fits what Paul was communicating—that Jesus became a slave, emptying himself of all but love, even life itself.

This set of verses is thought to be an early Christian hymn, addressing one of the church's most hallowed theologies—the divine condescension of Christ. As the hymn depicts, although one with God, Jesus voluntarily gave up His divine attributes to become one with man—He condescended. This self-renunciation is illustrated in the slave, or servant, analogy. Yet Christ's voluntary humiliation did not stop with the incarnation. It culminated in the stripping of all human dignity at the crucifixion, where He emptied himself of life. It was love that propelled His humiliation.

Often we appeal to our rights when justifying bad behavior. We have a "right" to make our own choices, to defend ourselves, to retaliate. If you want to make media headlines, just accuse someone of violating your human rights. We have become so wrapped up in our rights that many of us, even many Christians, have forgotten that the greatest man who ever walked this earth gave up His rights. If we are to follow in His footsteps, we must learn to set aside our rights, to serve others with humility, and to accept the suffering that comes with slavery.

📖 Repeatedly, Paul exhorts his readers to follow his example and that of Christ's. Read Romans 1:1, where Paul refers to himself as a slave to Christ. Some translations use the word servant instead of slave, but I believe slave better captures the question he is asking. Are you and I yielded to Christ as slaves, emptied of all rights of our own, owing all to the one to whom we belong?

📖 Paul goes a step further and calls his very life a libation. Read Philippians 2:17–18.

This metaphor is taken from the sacrificial ritual when wine was poured out at the foot of the altar to accompany a burnt, fellowship, or grain offering. Paul says the faith of the Philippians was their sacrifice and Paul's own life the libation poured out on their sacrifice. You or I might be called to sacrifice our lives, but most of us will be called to sacrifice only the things of life. May our sacrifices be a cause for celebration among our brothers and sisters in Christ.

📖 Paul next gives a word of warning. Read it in Philippians 3:2.

He is warning against Judaizers, those who believed Jewish Christians must also follow the Law of Moses. As we've already learned, Jews once slandered Gentiles by calling them dogs; now Paul reverses that contemptuous name-calling—the Judaizers are now the dogs. Paul further diminishes these antagonistic Jews by using the Greek word *katatome*, translated in English as "concision," or *"those who mutilate the flesh,"* but in verse 3 Paul goes on to say, *"For it is we who are the circumcision,"* those marked as God's.

Further on in his letter, Paul once again challenges his readers to imitate him. He contrasts the example of his life to the ways of the enemies of God.

📖 Read Philippians 3:17–21.

We have become so wrapped up in our rights that many of us, even many Christians, have forgotten that the greatest man who ever walked this earth gave up His rights.

Enemies of God seek to serve their own appetites rather than the needs of others. These particular enemies interpreted freedom in Christ as being freedom from all moral restraint. Their god was the belly, a symbol of sensual indulgences. Paul adamantly rejects this lie and reaffirms our citizenship in the kingdom of God. In verse 21, what does Paul say will happen to our humiliation?

_____

Just as Christ's humiliation resulted in His glorification, when you and I deny ourselves, our humiliation here will one day be transformed into glory there. What a day that will be!

Until that day you and I have a choice. We can, like Paul, choose to live a kingdom life, whether chained to a dark prison cell or setting aside our own desires while serving those in need. We can appeal to our rights when demanding our way, or we can deny ourselves and take up the crosses we were meant to bear.

In your remaining time today, meditate upon the prophesy of the suffering servant in Isaiah 53, which the hymn in Philippians 2 is based upon. As you read it, ask yourself how you can imitate such love.

MYSTERY SOLVED

Do you like a good mystery? Fine mysteries provide clues along the way but don't give the whole picture until the very end. They also toss in some turns to throw us off, so when the mystery is finally revealed, we say, "Ohhh, I missed that!" Just like in a good mystery, God gave the real clues all along, but many people missed them. In fact, Paul explains the whole mystery because so many had missed the clues.

📖 Read Colossians 1:25—2:5. What was the mystery?

_____

_____

_____

Paul was imprisoned for explaining the mystery, yet he continued to preach this message from his cell. The message, although not new, was new to most because they were just beginning to see how the clues added up to equal a God who dwelled in believing men and women.

Today we toss that concept around as if it were an old, worn-out pair of shoes. No longer are we stunned by it. We take it for granted and no longer stand in awe. But think about it. This was an earthshaking, ground-moving event. The great I AM is now taking up residence in mortal man. Christ in you! What a twist. Then to top it off, verse 6 declares the Gentiles to be coheirs with the Jews. This was indeed the greatest aha! moment. Paul is asking, "Do you get it?" Well, do you? If this reality were to truly sink in, how would it affect your witness?

_____

_____

_____

If we don't allow the reality of Christ living within us to become a game changer, then what Paul has to say next doesn't really matter—Christ doesn't matter; that is the reality of it. Statistics tell us that Christians are no better than the rest of the population when it comes to adultery, promiscuity, lying, cheating, broken marriages, abuse, and the list could go on. Why is that? Could it be that the reality of the Lord God moving into the hearts of His people is simply a concept? If it became a truth that each of us accepted, how much different would those statistics be?

Once that reality has set in and changed the way you view the daily choices before you, how do you make the change in your habits? Colossians 3 is the how-to chapter for holy living. Once again Paul returns to the image of clothing.

📖 Read Colossians 3:1–17. What are we to clothe ourselves in?

_____

_____

_____

Simply put, we may not always feel compassionate or patient, but we must choose to act this way. Likewise, we might feel angry or greedy, but we must choose to rid our hearts of these things. In our own power, we cannot do this. But because we've already established the reality that God lives within us, we can do all things. This is holy living. This is kingdom living.

Especially when we work with those outside the faith, we need be mindful that eyes are watching and ears are hearing us.

📖 Read Colossians 4:5–6. What must our conversations with outsiders be full of (NIV)? _____

Grace is like the atmosphere at a fine restaurant: it sets the stage for the meal to come. Salt makes the meal tasty and entices others to want more. When we are among non-Christians, grace and acceptance must fill our countenances, and the salt of love, compassion, and understanding fill our conversations.

We will wrap up our look at Paul's parables with three parable pictures from First Thessalonians. Paul wrote his letters to this community to strengthen their faith and give them hope in the face of persecution.

📖 Paul's love for this community is evident in 1 Thessalonians 2:7–8. What is this image?

_____

_____

Paul, Silas, and Timothy brought the gospel to the church at Thessalonica about two years prior during Paul's second missionary journey. The image

> _Grace is like the atmosphere at a fine restaurant: it sets the stage for the meal to come. Salt makes the meal tasty and entices others to want more._

of a nursing mother shows the tenderness with which these men cared for their young flock.

📖 A little further on in the letter, Paul writes the words in 1 Thessalonians 2:11–12.

If you've been blessed with a nurturing, encouraging, and comforting pastor, consider writing a letter expressing your gratitude for the sacrifices made as they've poured their lives into their church families, often at great cost to their own lives and personal ambitions.

At the close of his letter, Paul seems to throw several parable images into one final breath. He begins by addressing the question asked by Christians since the resurrection, How long must we hold on?

📖 Read Paul's answer in 1 Thessalonians 5:1–11. Make a list of all of the parabolic images used in these verses.

_____

_____

_____

_____

_____

No one knows the day or time when the Lord Jesus will return. With the *"thief in the night"* reference, Paul harkens back to the Parable of the Strong Man. Christ's return will take place suddenly, like the appearance of labor pains. A woman knows she's pregnant and that the baby is due. Likewise, we know Jesus will return, so the onset of labor pains should not catch us unprepared.

We are children of the light; thieves don't come in the daylight, they come under cover of darkness. Again, we should not be surprised, because Jesus told us He was coming back to take us home. Until that day comes, we ought to be busy doing good (*"be sober"* is analogous to not wasting our talents), living in faith and love with hope in our hearts. Furthermore, the breastplate is worn over the heart, where faith and love are generated, and the helmet is worn over the mind, where salvation is comprehended and accepted.

How are you preparing for the onset of labor pains? What are you doing to ready yourself and those you love for the coming day of the Lord? Make those steps concrete and record them here.

_____

_____

_____

_____

_____

_____

_____

Notes

The Best of the Rest

PARABLES FROM THE APOSTLES JAMES, PETER, JOHN, AND JUDE

GO AND DO LIKEWISE

The Best of the Rest

DAY ONE

As the brother of Jesus, James would have learned Jesus' parabolic ways firsthand. However, what we find in this letter from the leader of the Jerusalem church is not parables per say but parabolic figures of speech.

With passion and conviction, James addresses the problem of lukewarm Christianity. It is easy to say you believe and trust in the Lord, Jesus Christ, but quite another to live that faith out.

📖 James begins with a simple simile. Read James 1:5–8 in the New International Version and fill in the blanks.

Because he who doubts is like _____ , blown and tossed by the wind.

The context is the persecution that had begun after the stoning of Stephen. Christians in Jerusalem were afraid, and some worried they might not be able to make wise and godly choices if they were arrested. As their pastor, James was seeking to assure and inspire these new converts. He tells them wisdom is available if only they will ask. Then he cautions they also must take hold of that wisdom with boldness and confidence, trusting in the goodness and faithfulness of God—a mind that wavers in these situations is one not fully trusting in God's provision. When push comes to shove, when life is confronted by death and the waves come crashing down on us, where we place our trust is evidenced in our grace under pressure or our lack thereof.

Can you think of a time of crisis when you pushed aside doubt and held fast to your faith? Describe that time.

_____

_____

_____

In the next verses it is important to understand the implied simile. James is not saying rich people will wither and fade away—that would be counter to Jesus' teachings. But when viewed alongside the previous simile, we can see James is seeking to grab the attention of his wealthy members.

📖 Read James 1:9–11. If James is not saying wealthy people will wither and fade, what will fade away?

_____

_____

The fact that James does not sugarcoat this reality in the believer's life has reassured many going through trials and temptations. James wants to be certain we place the blame for temptation where it belongs.

📖 Read James 1:12–15. Where does James place the blame?

_____

_____

Satan is the one who tempts, but he uses our desires to entrap us. James compares a life being conceived in the womb to the evil desires within our hearts conceiving sin. If not aborted, that sin will continue to grow; when mature, it gives birth to the death of our soul. This process is seen in the lives of those who, perhaps when young and unknowing, choose to indulge the desires of the flesh (worldly pleasures). That indulgence leads to more sinful behavior, and the multitude of sinful behaviors slowly grows to consume the whole heart, mind, and soul, eventually leading to the death of that soul. The caution here is to be aware of the trap our fleshly desires can set for us. In the list below, mark those fleshly desires that are a weak area for you.

❏ Needing approval
❏ Needing love
❏ Needing acceptance
❏ Needing compassion
❏ Needing companionship
❏ Needing sexual fulfillment
❏ Needing security
❏ Needing escape from pressures
❏ Needing escape from past

Ask God to help you recognize when Satan is playing upon one of these needs. Ask Him to help you stand strong against Satan's ploys and to look to God to fill these needs as only He can.

James 1:16–18 continues with encouragement that God can be trusted. James wants his readers to recognize that when they see good in their lives, it is evidence of God's provision.

> *James compares a life being conceived in the womb to the evil desires within our hearts conceiving sin. If not aborted, that sin will continue to grow; when mature, it gives birth to the death of our soul.*

📖 Read these verses and write what James is comparing us to.

_____

_____

_____

The Jewish Christians in Jerusalem would have understood James's reference to firstfruits as stemming from Deuteronomy 26:9–11.

📖 Read this passage and explain what the Israelites were to do and why.

_____

_____

_____

In comparing new Christians to firstfruits, James is saying they were the first of a huge crop to come, and their presence—and even ours today—is a cause for praise to the God of the harvest. For all good things, including the faith of new believers, is a good and perfect gift from God. When new faith is born into a heart, are you bringing an offering of praise to the Lord for His goodness and grace, or are you more focused on the overwhelming sins in this world?

James might have created the original Nike slogan "Just do it," which summarizes this next section. Knowing what God says is one thing, but doing it is where the action is.

📖 Read James 1:22–25. Fill in the blanks in this paraphrase of the simile:

The one who hears the word but does not do it is like _____ _____ and afterwards forgets what he looks like.

What does James say the man who desires blessings must do?

_____

_____

Salvation frees us from sin's control. Freedom is the hallmark of a Christian's life.

Salvation frees us from sin's control. Freedom is the hallmark of a Christian's life. Living a kingdom life is freely doing what we've been taught. How are you applying and doing what this study has taught you?

_____

_____

_____

_____

_____

_____

_____

_____

BELIEVING IS DOING

The second chapter of James contains two parables that are perhaps the closest to those of Jesus when compared to those of the other apostles. Chapter 2 begins by addressing the thorny issue of favoritism. Today we might call this particular sin discrimination, partisanism, or cronyism. As we've already seen, society at this time was very much stratified. And how one received guests—and even who they received—moved people up and down this social ladder.

📖 Read James 2:1–13. What law is James calling the royal law?

_____

_____

_____

How does applying the royal law negate the negative effects of favoritism?

_____

_____

_____

Fill in the blanks for this summary statement from verse 13:
_____ triumphs over _____ .

James continues with another parable in this next section, which contain his most famous words, *"Faith without works is dead."* Read James 2:14–18. Kind words spoken to the naked and hungry are akin to platitudes offered to those who mourn. You know the words; they ring hollow even as they drip from our tongues:

"I'm so sorry, but God must have something better for you."
"Please, just call me whenever you need anything."
"I'm sorry for your loss, but now you can move on."

Words ring hollow without actions. We can confess anything, but actions require time, sacrifice, and commitment—the essence of faith. When I learned this lesson, I worked hard at ridding my vocabulary of such meaningless words. Not that offering caring and compassionate words are inappropriate, but perhaps are insufficient and too easy to simply slip from our tongues without much thought. Instead, when someone I know suffers loss, I now look for concrete actions I can take. I look for opportunities to demonstrate my love, empathy, and compassion. Anyone can offer platitudes. Only those who belong to Christ can offer His love. What changes will you make when comforting someone?

_____

_____

_____

_____

> **Kind words spoken to the naked and hungry are akin to platitudes offered to those who mourn.**

📖 Next James addresses a difficult issue, namely the untamed tongue. Read James 3:1–12 and fill in the blanks.

The body is controlled by a _____ in the mouth.
The tongue, like a _____ on a ship, can control our bodies.
Our tongues can set the whole body on _____, blessing or cursing.
From the mouth flows either _____ water or _____ , for salt water cannot yield fresh.

James does not mince words when speaking about the tongue running wild and untamed. He uses several images to make his point. If you and I want to live victorious lives, we must learn to control our tongues. How do we do this? Again, we are back to the premise with which James began—believing is not enough, we must do what we believe. When it comes to the tongue, we must apply the bit of God's Word and use the rudder of wisdom to steer. We must set the fire of God's Holy Spirit to purify what comes from our mouths, because what we say can have eternal consequences.

James has been encouraging his parishioners to live a life worthy of the kingdom calling they have received and answered. He's encouraged humility and invited them to act justly towards others. He's encouraged perseverance and asked them to bridle their tongues so what they believe, speak, and do will be in agreement with their kingdom calling. Now that he has built them up, he appeals to their sense of invincibility. Read James 4:13–17.
We make plans, but unless those plans are centered on what God desires, those plans and our lives will return void, for we do not know what tomorrow will bring or even if tomorrow will be. Therefore, every minute of every day ought to be numbered according to God's plans. My grandmother used to say she would do this or that "if the Lord be willing." I think that is a wonderful way to approach all our plans.

To close, James turns his attention once more to the rich. When you read James 5:1–9, what parables of Jesus come to your mind?

_____

_____

_____

_____

Several come to my mind: the parables of the lost treasures, the Parable of the Laborers in the vineyard, and the Parable of the Wheat and Tares.

James wants the rich to know their wealth is worthless in this kingdom. and how they treat their hired help, although acceptable in the world, is not acceptable by kingdom values. We are to be different. Our values and rules are at times even contradictory to what the world esteems. As subjects in the kingdom of God, we are to be patient, long-suffering, compassionate, and merciful.

The Church of the Holy Sepulcher in the Holy Land currently sits on the site where the Christian community of Jerusalem met to worship with James. According to historians Eusebius and Socrates Scholasticus, this church held worship services at Jesus' tomb and the site of the resurrection until 66 AD when Jerusalem fell. Today the teachings of its first pastor ring down through the ages and through the caretakers of this sacred site, calling all the world to live boldly, not only believing what has been taught but also doing what one believes.

THE ROCK CRIES OUT

The great persecution under Emperor Nero had begun. Throughout the Roman Empire, Christians were being rounded up, tortured, and killed for their faith. Unfortunately, most of the suffering came at the hands of fellow Jews, religious leaders, and even the believers' own families. While in Rome, Peter learned that the church in Jerusalem was being scattered throughout the Mediterranean world because of the intense persecution. Christians were frightened and many were losing faith. The two letters we have from Peter were written to this scattered church and contain words of wisdom, hope, and yes, parables.

📖 Peter begins by weaving a parabolic metaphor into his explanation of the saving work of Jesus Christ. Read 1 Peter 1:15–21. Did you catch it? What is the image?

_____

_____

_____

A bond slave was *"ransomed"* or redeemed when someone paid the debt owed by that slave—an image implied by the use of the word ransomed. Perhaps we've become too familiar with these words to fully comprehend the image that was created, but to suggest that the Son of God would stoop to pay what a debtor owed was absurd. It was also gracious beyond explanation. For each of us was a slave to sin, and Christ bought our freedom, not with tangible things like silver or gold, but with His own precious blood.

What does 1 Peter 1:23 say we have been born of, and not born of?

_____

_____

_____

What is this imperishable or incorruptible seed? _____

It is the living, breathing Word of God. The Bible you are studying is not simply another book. It contains the words of God enlivened in our hearts by the Holy Spirit, who is one with God the Father and Jesus, the Living Word. This is the imperishable and incorruptible seed planted within us when we open our hearts to Jesus. Peter reminds us by quoting Isaiah 40:6–8 that without this seed, we are like what?

_____

_____

The Bible you are studying is not simply another book. It contains the words of God enlivened in our hearts by the Holy Spirit, who is one with God the Father and Jesus, the Living Word.

Grass and flowers wither and fade, just as our perishable bodies will. But because the imperishable seed, Jesus Christ, is implanted within us, we will endure forever with the Lord. Is there someone you know who needs to be encouraged by these words? Make it a point to share them this week. If that person is you, write 1 Peter 1:23–25 on an index card and place it where it will remind you of this great promise.

Read 1 Peter 2:1–3. What is the pure spiritual milk we are to crave? (This one is hard, but the clues are in these verses.)

_____

_____

_____

_____

If we can taste and see that the Lord is good, the pure spiritual food must be the Word of God. We must hunger for God's Word. The living Word of God, Jesus, is the opposite of the things listed in verse 1. Can you identify what might be the opposite characteristic of those listed?

The opposite of malice is _____ .
The opposite of guile (deceit) is _____ .
The opposite of insincerity (hypocrisy) is _____ .
The opposite of envy is _____ .
The opposite of slander is _____ .

We are to put aside these sinful things and in their place cultivate goodness, honesty, authenticity, selflessness, and praise. Peter made it clear that we do this by drinking in the Word of God, which has the power to build strong spiritual muscles and bones. The Word of the Lord is good. Do you crave God's Word?

As Peter turns his attention to the fellowship of believers, he summarizes and blends what Jesus taught and what he no doubt heard Paul preach. What are the members of God's church like, according to Peter?

Read 1 Peter 2:4–5.

_____

_____

The people of God are living stones forming a spiritual house with Christ as our foundation and cornerstone. When you say you are a Christian, do you think of yourself as one stone in a huge cathedral pointing others toward God? Or do you think of yourself as a single stone?

Continue reading 1 Peter 2:9–10.

Together we form a royal priesthood, offering ourselves as daily sacrifices. Do you see the sacrifices you must make in order to fully follow God as a witness to the world? Is your witness one that draws people to God or pushes them away?

While at the same time we are a royal priesthood, we are also aliens and exiles.

We are to put aside these sinful things and in their place cultivate goodness, honesty, authenticity, self-lessness, and praise. Peter made it clear that we do this by drinking in the Word of God, which has the power to build strong spiritual muscles and bones.

📖 Read 1 Peter 2:11. How are we aliens and exiles?

_____

_____

We are exiles from another kingdom, and while we live here on this earth, which has its own king, we are aliens. We do not belong to this world. Verses 11–17 tell us how we are to behave as aliens. Remember, this letter was written to the scattered church, under much persecution. These would not have been simple instructions. Unfortunately, we have not taken these verses seriously. We've not conducted ourselves honorably among unbelievers. They witness us bucking authority as much as anyone else, and they see us use our freedom as an excuse to do what even they know is wrong. We are not honorable and therefore do not bring God glory.

📖 Read through these verses again, making note of what you must do as an alien and exile so you might bring glory to God.

_____

_____

_____

_____

_____

_____

> **We are exiles from another kingdom, and while we live here on this earth, which has its own king, we are aliens.**

The Best of the Rest

DAY FOUR

THE ROCK STANDS

Tucked within Peter's instructions to husbands and wives is a wonderful little parable illustration. It is concerning the adornments women wear.

📖 Read 1 Peter 3:1–7 and answer the question.

With what are women supposed to adorn their inner selves?

_____

_____

With what are men supposed to adorn their inner selves?

_____

_____

A wife is to dress her inner self with a gentle and peace-filled spirit, living in harmony with her husband. Likewise, a husband is to dress himself in loving consideration of his wife, showing her honor and deference. Note Peter doesn't say, "If the other person behaves properly." If all Christian couples dressed this way each morning, what an example we would be to the world! Women, list one way in which you can dress in peace and gentleness, and men, name one way you can show loving consideration and honor to your wives.

_____

_____

_____

📖 Further on, Peter gives instructions to those who *"tend the flock."* Read 1 Peter 5:1–4. To which parable of Jesus is Peter making reference?

_____

_____

_____

📖 Echoes of the Parable of the Good Shepherd fill this chapter. Elders are to emulate the Good Shepherd as they tend their own flocks, humbly going about their tasks. Read verses 6–8. What is the evil one doing?

_____

_____

Satan is always present, prowling around like a lion, looking to devour his prey. What is the shepherd's flock to do? Read verses 9–11.

_____

_____

_____

God promises that if you stand steadfast in your faith, trusting in the protection of the Good Shepherd, He will restore, support, strengthen, and establish you. There is one little word inserted in this promise that, once you have been through persecution of your own, you will know to be true. That word is *himself*. Christ, *himself*, will give you these things. The closest and most precious time I've ever spent with the Lord has been after I suffered persecution at the hands of wolves in sheep's clothing. I do not wish to go through that pain again, but I am almost willing so that I might experience the sweetness of His presence again. God is indeed with the lowly, the oppressed, the poor, and the persecuted. Peter knew this truth in a personal way, and he would experience it again, as he would soon be crucified at the hands of Nero. Take time now to pray for those who are suffering persecution around the world. Pray that they may experience the presence of Jesus in tangible ways.

After reminding his readers that he was an eyewitness to events in Christ's life and can therefore testify to their truthfulness, Peter paints one of the more beautiful word pictures of the risen Christ.

📖 Read about it and the trustworthiness of the written Word in 2 Peter 1:19–21.

There is only one other Scripture reference to Christ as the morning star.

Read this confession in Revelation 22:16. Who is the bright morning star?

_____

Did You Know?

PERSECUTED CHURCH

According to the World Evangelical Alliance, over 200 million Christians in at least 60 countries are persecuted every year and denied fundamental human rights solely because of their faith.

With the guidance of the Holy Spirit, we can know God's ways, and when we know His ways, we'll know our way.

This tells us that until Christ returns and shines His morning light into all dark places, forever banishing the darkness, we must use the Word of God illumined by the Holy Spirit to guide and direct us. I've written a book titled *Direction: Discernment for the Decisions of Your Life* because I was confused about spiritual discernment and how to know God's will. There are a lot of teachings out there and a lot of misinformation, so I went on a search for answers. What I've found is that in Christ there is no confusion. With the guidance of the Holy Spirit, we can know God's ways, and when we know His ways, we'll know our way.

For those who misdirect God's people, who teach false doctrine and propagate heresies, Peter delivers harsh words and some terrifying parabolic images.

📖 Read 2 Peter 2 and fill in the blanks.

Those who slander the Lord are like (v. 12) _____ .
They are _____ and _____ (v. 13).
They are an _____ brood (v. 14).
They are _____ and
_____(v. 17).
They are _____ of depravity (v. 19).

Finally, what does the proverb quoted from Proverbs 26:11 mean?

_____

_____

_____

Peter is speaking about those who have learned about Christ, have had the opportunity to accept and receive salvation, but instead reject the truth and go back to their sinful ways. These people are like pigs that are washed and then go back to the mud. They would have been better off never having been washed, Peter says. This passage is not about those who wander and doubt. I've counseled many a parent who nightly prays for a wandering son or daughter. Let me be clear: wandering is not rejecting. Renouncing the name of Christ and leading others to do the same is what this chapter is talking about. If you have or know any wandering prodigals, write their names here.

_____

_____

Pray that God's ever-seeking hand is upon them, and pray they're not fooled by the kinds of people described in this chapter. Pray their wandering hearts will return home safely, where the Father will run to them and bring them in with fanfare.

The Best of the Rest

DAY FIVE

WITNESSES TO LOVE

The three short letters of 1, 2, 3 John were written by 'the disciple whom Jesus loved,' probably after the fall of Jerusalem. This was a dark time for the church. Christ had not returned as was expected, the temple was no longer standing, the faithful were scattered, and belief in Jesus the Messiah was waning. There is only one parabolic image in these three letters, but through the ages this one image has painted our view of God with a kaleidoscope of colors. What is this image?

📖 Read 1 John 1:5–7; 2:10–11. What is God?

_____

_____

_____

Light represents what is pure and holy. If you and I profess to be children of the light, we must also be pure and holy. Not "holier than thou," and not perfect as the world defines perfection, but pure of heart. When we have the light of God in us, darkness cannot hide there. If we have the light of God in us, little by little that light chases away the sin that hides in dark and secretive places. The light will expose our selfishness, our greed, and our hatred. What has God's light exposed in your own heart? Are you selfish or greedy? Do you harbor resentment or anger toward a brother or sister? Make note of it here, taking these sins into the light where they can be chased away.

_____

_____

_____

One more note about light. When light passes through another medium, it is said to refract or bend. When a prism receives light, it bends it into a spectrum of colors. When you and I receive the light of God, we refract that light, bending it toward a world that is dark and dreary. As reflectors and refractors of that light, we bring out the God-colors in this world. How are you bending God's light into, and bringing the God-colors out of, the world?

_____

_____

_____

Taken as a whole, John's letters reveal two complimentary characteristics of God. The first is that God is light, and the second is that God is love. When you love, you are shining God's light. When you and I love, we bring out the God-colors in the world.

It is appropriate that the letter from Jude, a brother of Jesus, is near the end of the Bible. It is an exhortation to believers to stand strong in their faith, to recognize false teachers, and to live God-shaped lives. It contains more metaphors from nature than any other New Testament book and is therefore a fitting end to our study of the parables in the epistles.

To understand Jude and the strength of his parabolic imagery, we must first understand the heresy confronting the church at this time. False teachers were claiming that Jesus came to bring special knowledge and revelation, available only to a select few through dreams and spiritual revelation. They minimized sin, focusing instead on the spiritual, with some even teaching that Jesus was merely human and only became divine through _gnosis_, a special knowledge. Gnosticism has once again reared its ugly head in the

> **When we have the light of God in us, darkness cannot hide there. If we have the light of God in us, little by little that light chases away the sin that hides in dark and secretive places.**

church today, claiming secret knowledge available only to an elect group of people. Jude's strong metaphors reminded the readers of his day as well as ours that judgment would come against false teachers and anyone who leads a believer astray.

 Jude begins by reminding his readers of those in Scripture who turned against the Lord and followed false teachers. Read Jude 1–11, noting the metaphors.

Everlasting chains (v. 6)
Eternal fire (v. 7)
Dreamers (v. 8)
Irrational, or unreasoning, animals (v. 10)

After the review of history, Jude turns his pointed metaphors toward those within the community of faith who seek to distort the teachings of Christ. Within verses 12–13, there are seven frightening metaphors. Identify them as you read.

Blemishes (v. 12)
Shepherds (NIV) (v. 12)
Waterless clouds (v. 12)
Trees without fruit (v. 12)
Uprooted and twice dead (v. 12)
Wild waves foaming shame (v. 13)
Wandering stars (v. 13)

In the early church, believers shared a meal, called a love feast, before taking part in the Lord's Supper. The men Jude is describing are sharing this love feast; they are members of the community of faith. Just because some are leaders in the church does not mean we can trust what they teach. These teachers claimed they possessed secret knowledge, but God's Word makes it clear that each of us can hear from God and possess all we need to be saved by faith. As Christians we must prove all teachings against the Word of God, passing all things through the Holy Spirit, who guides us in all truth. Finish reading this short yet powerful letter, noting a final metaphor, *"clothing stained by corrupted flesh"* (v. 23 NIV). What do you think it means?

_____

_____

This is the ancient form of "hate the sin but love the sinner." Jude tempers his damning rhetoric with the need to love. His letter is a reminder that righteous indignation is appropriate when aimed at the sin that so corrupts. But Jude also makes it clear we must not close the door on the sinner, for God's love is available to all, even at the last hour.

Is there someone you know who is covered in so much sin it is hard to separate the sin from the sinner? Does your blood boil with righteous indignation at the things this person says or does? Write that person's name here.

_____

Ask God to help you separate the sin from the sinner, to unconditionally love the sinner so he or she might return to the fold or meet Jesus for the first time.

Living Parables

EXAMPLES OF LIVING PARABLES

A NEW START

Living Parables

DAY ONE

We've looked at specific parables of Jesus in the Gospels and parabolic images and sequels from Paul and the disciples in the rest of the New Testament. In our final few days, we will look at parables in a broader sense. Some call these types, or symbols. I like to call them living parables, as they are living examples pointing to a deeper spiritual concept.

The second Adam is one such living parable image. The comparison between Adam and Christ occurs in Paul's writings principally in three texts—the hymn of Philippians (which we've already examined), 1 Corinthians 15, and Romans 5. Paul did not invent this comparison himself, for the hymn of Philippians was probably an early Christian hymn quoted by Paul. However, the second Adam parable, as Paul explains it, is one that has shaped the church's understanding and interpretation of Christ's life and death from the time of Paul forward. For that reason we will take a closer look.

📖 Let's begin with Romans 5:12–14. Fill in the blank from verse 14:

Adam is a _____ of the one to come.

The word *therefore* at the beginning of this passage directs us to look at what has come before. Paul has just given his readers a history lesson. Beginning with the first chapter of Romans, he outlines the dire situation we are in because of our rebellion. But Paul assures us that God is faithful and asks only our faithfulness in return. Then in chapter 4, Paul gives his most compelling argument for justification by faith, an argument in which he uses another parable that we will look at tomorrow. In chapter 5 he delivers the climax of the story. In storytelling we call this a circle ending, because the end brings us back to, or circles us around to, the beginning.

📖 Continue reading Romans 5:15–17.

As Paul puts it, Adam's single sin led to many sins (v. 12) and brought the reign of death to all people. Paul makes it clear it is not the breaking of the law that brought death, for death was already present before Moses delivered the law in the form of the Ten Commandments. It was the introduction of sin at the fall that brought death into God's perfect creation. One man and one woman opened that door. In the biggest reversal of all time, it was one man, Jesus, born of a woman, who opened the door for all to receive life.

📖 Finish reading this amazing parable explanation in Romans 5:18–21.

One man's selfishness was answered by another's selflessness. One man's self-righteousness was answered by another's righteousness. One man's disobedience was answered by another's obedience, even unto death, so we might have life. Once again Paul makes it clear that this has nothing to do with the law; the law merely made the situation undeniable. We could not save ourselves. There was no sacrifice big enough, pure enough, or holy enough until God chose, in grace and love, to offer His own sacrifice.

Paul furthers his assessment of Adam and Christ as a living parable in his answer to the question to the Corinthians about resurrection. Some were asking whether there will be a physical resurrection or if it will simply be a spiritual one.

📖 Read Paul's answer in 1 Corinthians 15:42–49 and summarize it here.

_____

_____

_____

_____

The first Adam became a living being; the second became a life-giving spirit. We were born of man (Adam's inheritance) in earthly bodies corrupted by sin, so shall we be born again of another man (Christ) into a spiritual body made incorruptible by Christ's righteousness. Our mortality is replaced with immortality. Because of the great gift of the second Adam, Jesus Christ, who conquered death on our behalf, the perishable is clothed once and for all with the imperishable.

In theological terms this is called recapitulation. It is when the head of the human race has been replaced or "re-headed," which is the exact meaning of the word recapitulation. The theology plays out this way: once Adam, the head of the human race, tainted all who followed because of his sinfulness; now Christ, the head of the new humanity, covers all who follow with His righteousness. No longer are you and I bound by the lineage of sin that was our inheritance from Adam. We are heirs to a new promise. As you think

One man's selfishness was answered by another's selflessness. One man's self-righteousness was answered by another's righteousness. One man's dis- obedience was answered by another's obedience, even unto death, so we might have life.

about this inheritance, how does it change the way you see yourself, your family history, and your future?

_____

_____

_____

Regardless of your family history and even your own past, because of Christ's recapitulation your life has a new beginning, a new start. What does this mean for you?

_____

_____

_____

As a closing today, reread the hymn in Philippians 2:6–11 as a song of praise. Use this opportunity to thank God for the way He completed and perfected the pattern begun in Adam, that through His willingness to become one with us, He has taken our past and given it a new beginning.

A Promise and a Blessing

As we said yesterday, Paul uses Romans 1–4 to prepare for his climatic parable, that of the first and second Adam. However, just before that, in chapter 4, Paul gives another living parable illustration—that of the faith of Abraham.

Before we read this wonderful faith illustration, we must understand how significant the patriarch Abraham was to the Jewish people but how distorted his legacy had become. He was the father of the Jewish nation, and it was because of his acts of faithfulness that the Jewish people were God's people. However, the slide wasn't too far down the slippery slope from having pride in Abraham's acts to seeing his acts as the reason for God's blessings. Some of us were taught to relate to God this way. We grew up in strict homes, were told "God is watching you" and "He's going to punish you if you don't behave." Is this your view of God? Do you see Him, or treat Him, as a spiritual Santa Claus, handing out desired gifts or lumps of coal depending upon your behavior?

There is a fine line between our actions extracting blessings from God and God blessing us because we've obeyed. In Paul's day, some new Christians were blending this distorted belief of God with their faith in Christ and His emphasis on doing good things for others.

📖 With this background, read Romans 4:1–12

Paul quotes Genesis 15:6 to make his point that Abraham was accepted by God because of his faith and not because of his obedience to the law, which had not yet been given. In fact, the requirement of circumcision does not come until 430 years later, as recorded in Genesis 17.

> *As Paul says so beautifully in this living parable from the life of Abraham, our faith, like that of Abraham's, can be credited to our account. That faith is more valuable than our sin is weighty, and when placed on God's scales, the faith side is always more.*

Note that Genesis doesn't say Abraham was righteous but that his faith was credited or reckoned to him as righteousness. You and I will never measure up to God's holy standard. We cannot. Regardless of how we might try, our humanity will always get in our way. But as Paul says so beautifully in this living parable from the life of Abraham, our faith, like that of Abraham's, can be credited to our account. That faith is more valuable than our sin is weighty, and when placed on God's scales, the faith side is always more.

📖 Read Romans 4:13–16. If it is not by acts or works, how does righteousness come to us (v. 16)?

_____

_____

_____

It is a gift of grace received by faith. It bothers me when I hear even good biblical scholars say that the Old Testament is all about the law and the New Testament is all about grace. I want to shout, "No, have you not read Paul?" Sometimes this chapter of Romans is referred to as the justified-by-faith chapter, but I like to call it the saved-by-grace-from-the-beginning-of-time chapter. Because that is what Paul is saying. He wants us to know that beginning with Abraham, it was God's grace that justified. It was God's grace that used a flawed man like Abraham to father a nation. It was God's grace that formed a people into the nation of Israel in spite of their faithlessness, and it was God's grace that sent His only Son to show the world what true faithfulness is. His faithfulness can be ours as a gift of grace, if only we will receive it.

📖 Paul summarizes it in his letter to the Galatians. Read Galatians 3:5–9. How do we become *"children of Abraham"* (NIV)?

_____

_____

_____

If we rely upon the grace of God received by faith, we are a part of the blessing given Abraham. What is that blessing (v. 8)?

_____

_____

That all the world would be blessed is the blessing of Abraham, which now flows through you and through me. We are to be God's blessings in the world. This is what kingdom people are called to do and be; it is our mission. Have you thought about yourself as a blessing? What can you do today to be a blessing from God to your neighbors, your co-workers, your community, your family?

_____

_____

_____

_____

Besides being God's blessings in the world, we also have another significant role illustrated by Paul using a familiar image—that of a seed. Unfortunately, in some translations the word *seed* has been replaced with the word *offspring*, a translation that, in my opinion, loses some of its flavor.

📖 Read this promise in Galatians 3:15–29, paying special attention to verses 15, 16, 29. And if your translation uses the word *offspring*, try inserting *seed* and see how this changes the meaning for you. Then answer the questions.

Who were the promises made to? _____

Who is the seed or offspring? _____

If we belong to Christ, what does Paul call us? _____

How do we become heirs of this promise? _____

Through faith in Christ we become Abraham's seed and heirs to the promise God gave him thousands of years ago. That promise was that we would become a kingdom overflowing with blessings so we might in turn bless others. It is significant that we are a simple seed. A seed must be watered and nourished to become what it is to be. A seed starts small and grows larger as it puts down roots. A seed carries the DNA of what it is supposed to be when it is fully mature. We are indeed a seed of what we will one day be. Our kingdom is immature and not yet what it will one day become when Jesus comes to reign forever. How are you nurturing the seed within you? How is your community of faith nurturing the seeds among you?

_____

_____

_____

_____

_____

> *A seed must be watered and nourished to become what it is to be. A seed starts small and grows larger as it puts down roots. A seed carries the DNA of what it is supposed to be when it is fully mature. We are indeed a seed of what we will one day be.*

Living Parables

THE LIVING PARABLE EVENT

Easter in its earliest beginnings was the combination of two celebrations—a Jewish (*Pascha* or Passover) and the Christian (Resurrection Day or Lord's Day).[4] The early Christians found it highly pertinent that Jesus was crucified on the Passover, the exact same day of the month when the Exodus Passover took place in Egypt. For them, and for us, this became a living parable event in which the deliverance from the bondage of Egypt was a type of redemption from sin later fulfilled in the cross. In fact, early Jewish Christians celebrated Easter by celebrating the Exodus from Egypt with the Sedar meal, just like Jesus did at the Last Supper, but celebrated it as a fulfilled promise through Christ's death and resurrection. Early Christians pointed to several events from Jesus' life to make their case. We will look at a few of these.

📖 First, read John 1:29. What declaration did John make about Jesus?

_____

_____

📖 Read 1 Peter 1:18–19. Who does Peter claim Jesus to be?

_____

_____

_____

In the Exodus Passover, the blood of a spotless lamb was required. When this lamb's blood was smeared across the lintel and doorposts, it allowed the angel of death and judgment to pass over those living inside that house. Jesus was our spotless, sinless, lamb. When His blood was smeared over an ugly cross, it covered our sin, allowing death and judgment to pass over us. Hebrews 10:1 explains it this way. Underline the words *shadow* and *realities*.

> *The law is only a shadow of the good things that are coming—not the realities themselves. For this reason it can never, by the same sacrifices repeated endlessly year after year, make perfect those who draw near to worship* (NIV).

The first Passover was a parable or shadow of the law as it demonstrated in graphic form the ultimate penalty for sin and the only remedy for it. But as this passage makes clear, this was only to be a parable or foreshadow of a new reality that was to come. Endlessly repeated sacrifices were never supposed to be the final word, for they would never suffice to make us perfect, to stand holy and pure before God. This living parable event only pointed toward the reality that was to come. That reality is Jesus. He was the one and only true spotless lamb whose blood could cover our sins.

📖 Likewise, our creation is a shadow or parable of what is to come. Read Genesis 1:26–27. In your Bible, highlight the word *image*.

📖 Now read Hebrews 2:6–9. What was our creation pointing toward?

_____

_____

_____

Did you catch that? We are parables, living parables, pointing to a new reality that was yet to come. We were made in the image of God to be pointers to someone greater than us, who would do what we were unable to do. Everything was made subject to us, but we were poor stewards. Praise God, He had a plan, a plan that was there from the beginning. The plan all along was Jesus. Tomorrow we will look at *the* parable, Jesus Christ.

Today's lesson is short because I want you to prepare for tomorrow's lesson by reading the beautifully poetic depiction of that living parable in John 1:1–14. Allow the words of John to penetrate your heart and mind as you think of Jesus as the greatest living parable that ever was.

> **We are parables, living parables, pointing to a new reality that was yet to come. We were made in the image of God to be pointers to someone greater than us, who would do what we were unable to do.**

Living Parables

DAY FOUR

THE GREATEST LIVING PARABLE

We have come to the culmination of our study. Over the last several weeks, we've looked at the parables as told by our Lord and those recorded in the Gospels. We've examined the parable images and sequels created by His followers. Finally, we've looked at the living parables in the lives of Adam and Abraham and the parabolic event of the Passover. All of these images, metaphors, and events were created for one reason—in some way to embody the one who is our living parable. Let us begin to unpack this concept beginning with Jesus' own words.

📖 Read John 14:8–11 and answer the question.

If we have seen Jesus, whom have we also seen? _____

📖 Now read 2 Corinthians 4:4.

Looking back to yesterday, we read that we were to be the image or parable of God, but we did not live up to our calling. Instead of reflecting God's glory, we fell from that glory. We fell so far that when the one who perfectly reflects that image came, we could not see Him.

📖 Read Colossians 1:15 (NIV) and fill in the blanks.
He is the _____ of the invisible _____, the _____ over all creation.

📖 Jesus Christ was the visible image of the invisible God. Read John 14:9 and write down what Christ said about anyone who has seen Him.

_____

_____

Through Christ we both see the Father and better grasp our purpose and potential. A major aspect of our goal in life is to attain God's character. Read Hebrews 1:3 and again in your Bible underline the word *image*.

In this verse *image* is translated from the Greek word *charakter*. This word means "a tool for [en]graving . . . 'a stamp' or 'impress,' as on a coin or seal, in which case the seal or die which makes an impression bears the 'image' produced by it, and, vice versa, all the features of the 'image' correspond respectively with those of the instrument producing it."[5]

The image is the character. Humanity was made in the image of God, the *imagio Dei* as theologians call it. Jesus, on the other hand, is preeminently the image of God. He is the one who is God's authoritative representative on earth, who speaks with God's voice, who perfectly reflects the character of God, and who is quite literally the face of God to humanity.

When we look at Jesus, we see the triune God. Jesus perfectly reflects who God is in character, in what He does, and how He interacts with others. We see the character of God when Jesus loves, becomes angry at injustice, and shows His hatred toward sin and hypocrisy. Jesus also shows us God's compassion and mercy when His heart breaks at the suffering sin causes.

Add to this list other character qualities of God you can think of that Jesus represents.

_____

_____

_____

> *Jesus is the one who is God's authoritative representative on earth, who speaks with God's voice, who perfectly reflects the character of God, and who is quite literally the face of God to humanity.*

Jesus reflects God not only by who He is but also by what He does. When He calmed the storm, Jesus demonstrated God's power over nature and His dominion over the earth. When He sought out the lost and freed those who were held captive to demon possession, Jesus demonstrated God's compassion and mercy. He fed thousands, revealing God's provision, and included little children in His inner circle, showing God's tenderness.

What are some other ways Jesus reflected God by His actions?

_____

_____

_____

In His relationships with the disciples, Jesus mirrored God's patience and love for His children. In His relationship with the blind religious leaders of the day, He reflected God's wrath upon those who tolerate injustice.

In what other relationships did Jesus mirror God's relationship with us?

_____

_____

_____

> *It is only through the living parable who descended from His throne, clothed himself in human flesh, lived a sinless life, and demonstrated a depth of love we'd never seen that we could begin to comprehend our God.*

Without Jesus we would only have part of the picture of who God is and how He relates to us. Although the Old Testament is a true and accurate account of God's character, that depiction in us was distorted by our sin. We simply could not comprehend God's goodness, justice, and love. It is only through the living parable who descended from His throne, clothed himself in human flesh, lived a sinless life, and demonstrated a depth of love we'd never seen that we could begin to comprehend our God.

This is the story the Bible tells. Not only did Jesus come to complete a story that began with the love of His Father, Jesus came as the ultimate parable—a living, breathing Word—the climax of God's grand parable.

How does this idea of Jesus as a living parable who points us to God inform the way you see Jesus?

_____

_____

_____

Jesus is the parable of all parables. But the story doesn't end there . . .

Living Parables

DAY FIVE

LIVING THE KINGDOM OF GOD

We have come to our final day, and you might be saying, "What more could there be? After all, we've studied the parable of all parables, Jesus." You are right. There is none greater than He. But even Jesus did not leave the story there. The story is still being written, and we have a role to play.

At this point one might ask the question that the psalmist asks. Record the question from Psalm 8:4 here.

_____

_____

The bottom line is, we were given a role to play, and we blew it. So why would God include us in the resolution of His great drama? The answer lies not in us but in God.

📖 Read Ephesians 1:7. According to what are we given this second chance?

_____

_____

_____

Over and over again the Scriptures extol God's faithfulness. He keeps His covenants. God made a covenant with us, and regardless of whether we've broken our part of the deal, He will fulfill His. God's first covenant was demonstrated in our creation. As we've already examined, God created us for the purpose of His glory and God will not be thwarted from His goal.

So what is it that God wants us to do? I'll give you a hint: God's goal hasn't changed.

_____

_____

_____

📖 Read 2 Corinthians 3:13–24.

These words from Paul reference the account of Moses' encounter with God in Exodus 34:29–36. Read it and answer the question.

Why did Moses cover his face?

_____

_____

Paul is comparing the glory of God now seen through Jesus to when, in Moses' time, the Israelites could not look upon God's splendor because of His purity. Like mirrors, we were to reflect the radiance Moses saw in the face of God, but we could not. Our mirrors were cracked in the fall.

If you've ever tried to use a cracked mirror, you know how it distorts the reflection. No matter how hard we tried, the image of God we beheld was now distorted. If our mirrors had not been cracked, there would have been no need for the veil. But because we could not properly see and reflect that image, the veil was needed. Jesus came to fix our brokenness and remove the veil. Because it is not us that the world sees but Christ in us, no longer must we veil our faces. Our faces now fully reflect the God who is in us. With unveiled faces, as Paul puts it, we can once again reflect the Lord's glory. Yet Paul doesn't say we are a perfect reflection. Instead, he declares that those who behold the divine glory are participants in a process of transformation into that divine image, a process that is gradual and progressive.

If our mirrors had not been cracked, there would have been no need for the veil. But because we could not properly see and reflect that image, the veil was needed. Jesus came to fix our brokenness and remove the veil.

Read 1 Corinthians 15:48–49. Fill in the blank.

We will bear the image of the man of _____ .

We are to bear the image of the risen Christ, not simply as mere reflections but so that through living out the story of Christ, the world might be transformed. All of the parables we've studied were told for this reason—that we might become living parables to the world, just as Christ was for us. Thus, in our parable living we are participating in the building of the kingdom of God here on earth as it is in heaven. Said another way, through our kingdom living we are participating in God's mission to restore what had been broken and to finally do what we were created to do—reflect God's glory once again.

Read Romans 8:29. What is our job description?

_____

_____

But as 1 Corinthians 15:49 infers, our metamorphosis is not yet complete.

Read 1 Peter 1:14–16. What is the goal of this transformation process?

_____

_____

_____

> *This is the picture the parables paint. When we strive to live parable-shaped lives, little by little the trans- formation will take place, and we will become the living parables we were called to be—pure, righteous, and holy.*

We are called to holiness of heart and hand. That is a tall order, I know, but we have been given the tools to do it. After all, Christ lives in us! We won't simply snap our fingers and become holy. It is indeed a process. We are under construction from the inside out. If the word *holy* frightens you, try replacing it with the word *pure*. You and I are called to have pure hearts and pure motives in everything we say and do. This is the picture the parables paint. When we strive to live parable-shaped lives, little by little the transformation will take place, and we will become the living parables we were called to be—pure, righteous, and holy.

Read 1 Corinthians 15:20–23 to learn when that completion will take place. Record your answer here.

_____

_____

_____

Until that time, we are the keepers of the kingdom, and as subjects of this kingdom we must live in such a way as to please the King. This is the message all of the parables together point toward. In fact, it is the message of the story from the beginning. On that final day when Christ comes in His ultimate glory, our full glory (our holiness) and that of all creation will be completely restored. That is a story worth telling, a kingdom-building mission worth joining. It is a parable worth living.

Works Cited

1. *History of Herodotus, 440 BCE*, book 3, chapter 107.

2. Eugene Peterson, *Eat This Book* (Grand Rapids: Eerdmans Publishing, 2006), 82.

3. "Amazing Grace" (My Chains Are Gone) by Chris Tomlin (Universal Music Publishing Group, Sony/ATV Music Publishing LLC, EMI Music Publishing).

4. *History of the Christian Church AD 1-311 Ante-Nicene Christianity,* by Phillip Schaff (Oxford University 1884), 206–209.

5. *Vine's Expository Dictionary of Old and New Testament Words* by W. E. Vine (Thomas Nelson, 1996) "Image"

Notes

Notes

Notes

Notes

Notes

Notes

Notes

Notes

Notes

Notes

Notes

Notes

Notes

Notes